# ALAN SHAPIRO

# SELECTED POEMS
### 1974-1996

CARCANET

First published in 2000 by
Carcanet Press Limited
4th Floor, Conavon Court
12-16 Blackfriars Street
Manchester M3 5BQ

A CIP catalogue record for this book
is available from the British Library
ISBN 1 85754 466 8

The publisher acknowledges financial assistance
from the Arts Council of England

Set in 10pt Ehrhardt by Bryan Williamson, Frome
Printed and bound in England by SRP Ltd, Exeter

# Contents

Introduction (from 'Woodstock Puritan')                         7

from *Mixed Company* (1996)

The Letter                                                      27
My Mother and a Few Friends                                     29
Wife: Labor                                                     31
Isabel                                                          32
Night Terrors                                                   33
Single Mother                                                   34
Pleasure                                                        39
Lethe                                                           40
Soul                                                            41
The Friend                                                      42
In the Land of the Inheritance                                 47
Manufacturing                                                   51
The Basement                                                    54
The Fight                                                       57
Between Assassinations                                          58

from *Covenant* (1991)

The Sweepers                                                    61
Maison des Jeunes                                               62
Mud Dancing                                                     64
Virgil's Descent                                                66
Night Watch                                                     68
The Lesson                                                      70
Love Poem                                                       79
In the Kingdom of Pleasure                                      81
Separation of the Waters                                        82
Turn                                                            84
Home Movie                                                      85
Purgatory                                                       87
Covenant                                                        89

from *Happy Hour* (1987)

Happy Hour                                                      95
Genie                                                           96
Familiar Story                                                  97
The Riddle                                                      98

Christmas Story                                100
Rickshaw                                       102
Extra                                          104
Astronomy Lesson                               109

from *The Courtesy* (1983)

On the Eve of the Warsaw Uprising              113
The Courtesy                                   114
Yahrzeit                                       116
What Makes You Think It's Fear                 117
First Night                                    118
Love Letter                                    119
Moving Day                                     120
Harvesting                                     121

from *After The Digging* (1981)

Randolf Routh to Charles Trevelyan             125
The Dublin Evening Mail                         127
Captain Wynne to Randolf Routh                  128
Passage Out                                     130
Hands of Compassionate Women                    136
Night Seasons                                   138

I

For some mysterious reason, most of my friends in childhood and adolescence were from broken homes. In grade school, the kids I ran with – Saul Chessler, Stevie Goldstein, Michael Catt, and Gary O'Brien – were raised by single mothers, and they all went wonderful places and did exotic things on the weekends when their fathers visited. They went to movies, ball games, circuses, museums; in the summertime, they took day trips to the Cape, or to the north shore; they went camping and hiking in Maine, Vermont, New Hampshire. I, whose parents were thoroughly, if not happily, married, never went anywhere. Whatever fission of the early sixties split apart the nuclear family inside other people's houses became the glummest fusion of the fifties in my own. And as the weekends rolled around and my friends deserted me, with my mother down in the basement doing laundry all afternoon, and my father napping in the den before the droning television, it was hard not to think that life was a perpetual party, and only those kids got invited whose parents were divorced. I used to beg my parents to please get divorced, or separate at least, so I could go someplace for once, do something exciting. They'd laugh and pat me on the head and say, 'What a card, what a sense of humor.'

By the time I went to high school, I'd long since given up any hope of their divorcing, but I was still drawn to kids from broken homes. My closest friend in those years was Jeff Morrison. At the beginning of our freshman year, Jeff had moved to Brookline with his mother and his brothers, John and Bruce, after his parents got divorced. Even at fifteen, Jeff was a handsome, even manly-looking kid, dark-haired and muscular. But his apparent manliness was qualified, if not entirely undercut, by his utter guilelessness, his incapacity for deceit or dissimulation. He was kind-hearted and too trusting. He had an almost childlike faith in the goodness of other people, assuming everyone accepted him on his own terms as he accepted them on theirs. Though he never talked about his family or how the divorce affected him, I wonder now if his inveterate openness to others, his almost reckless refusal to think that anyone would do him harm, wasn't in some way a reaction to the pain and betrayal he may have felt about his absent father, his broken home, as if he thought the more remote somebody was to him, the more reliably familial that person was or ought to be. Though it confused and bewildered him when other kids would take advantage of his great good nature, or when adults would misinterpret his naïve honesty as disrespect, he was incapable of changing, of taking on a more guarded, more circumspect demeanor. His innate, unsophisticated decency seemed to prevent him from learning from experience.

But it wasn't just his innocence that made him vulnerable to others. Jeff also had about him a rather hapless air; he had a gift for getting himself into difficult and embarrassing situations. I discovered this soon after we met at tryouts for basketball. We both made the freshman team. The school supplied uniform and sneakers, but we had to purchase our own jockstraps. Jeff and I went to a local sporting-goods store. I bought a medium jockstrap, Jeff bought an extra large. Now I'd already seen him in the showers after tryouts, so I was a little surprised. He was well enough endowed, but an extra large? When I called him on this, he said, 'Didn't you see that beautiful chick at the cash register?' I said yeah, I saw her. So what? 'Well,' he said, 'I thought maybe if I got an extra large she might, you know, notice me.' She didn't, of course, and now he was stuck with a jockstrap that maybe the Jolly Green Giant could have worn, but certainly not Jeff. It looked more like an oxygen mask than a jockstrap. All that year, as we got dressed for games and practices, Jeff had to put up with merciless teasing from his teammates. Invariably somebody would pull on the baggy cup and call down into it, 'Anybody home?' 'My man, you got room in there for all the team equipment,' Dale Clark, one of the black kids, used to say, 'You suffering some serious delusions.' Jeff would laugh along with everybody else. He took the razzing in stride, submitted to it the way he submitted to life in general, with cheerful, even dignified acceptance.

Jeff was a good basketball player, serious on the court, hardworking, dogged, his face impassive, utterly without expression, whether he played well or poorly, whether his team won or lost. His interest and pleasure in the game seemed entirely intrinsic to the playing itself. He was intense without being competitive at all.

His attitude to the game couldn't have differed more from mine. By my freshman year, I was only just beginning to doubt my prospects for a career in professional basketball. In grade school I was something of a star. Physically and athletically, I bloomed early. In fact, I am now roughly the same height and weight I was when I was twelve years old, so back then I was bigger and more agile than almost everyone I played against. The men in my family, especially on my father's side, are rather tall. My father, himself a star in high school, used to tell me as I was growing up that I had big feet, I'd be taller than he was, and so if I only practiced hard enough, who knew with my big feet how good I'd get, how far I'd go. Unfortunately, while my peers continued growing, I was stuck at five foot eight, one hundred and fifty pounds. I went from power forward in sixth grade, to small forward in seventh, to big guard in eighth, and by high school

I was just a point guard, and a rather small point guard at that. Even now, some thirty years later, whenever he sees me my father always shakes his head and says, 'I can't understand it, Al, you had such big feet.'

Anyway, being highly competitive and emotional, someone whose pleasure on the court depended much more than it should have on winning and excelling, I was drawn to Jeff's detached attachment to the sport. His single-minded, unworldly devotion to just playing became a sort of laid-back, unambitious earth to the ether of my intense ambition.

By the summer between my junior and senior years, however, Jeff's peculiarities took a political form. This was the summer of 1969. Over the past year or so, we'd seen the Tet Offensive, the escalation of the antiwar movement at home, the assassinations of Martin Luther King, Jr., and Bobby Kennedy, the Democratic National Convention in Chicago, and widespread rioting in many inner cities. It embarrasses me to say this now but I followed these events from a safe distance, with only casual interest. My two obsessions, basketball and my girlfriend, Martha (in that order, I'm afraid), were all I cared about. I had my sights monomaniacally set on my senior year, when I would move into the starting lineup of the varsity team. But even if basketball hadn't so completely occupied my mind and heart, I doubt I would have joined the student-led antiwar movement. I was too cowed by my father in those days, too fearful of doing anything he'd disapprove of. Not that he was dictatorial or hypercritical. Far from it. In his eyes, I could do no wrong, especially as an athlete. If I had a bad game (and he came to all of them, even hitchhiking sometimes out to the remoter suburbs to see me play), it was the coach's fault for not utilizing my abilities, or my teammates' for not playing up to my level, or the officials' for favoring the other team. No matter how I played, he praised me, and the more he praised me, the more acutely I would feel the discrepancy between the player he imagined me to be and the player I knew I was. After a while I began to feel his disappointment was in direct proportion to his encouragement, his compliments a measure of my failure. The pressure of trying to justify his excessive faith in my abilities made me resent him even as it terrified me that I might let him down.

In reaction to the social turmoil taking place around us, I think he began to fear that I might throw away what I had worked so hard for. He grew more watchful, protective, and authoritarian than he normally was. We'd watch the nightly news at dinnertime, the latest body counts from Vietnam, the rioting at home, the demonstrations, marches, drug busts, and even though he was against the war, repeatedly he'd warn me that if I got involved in any protests he'd disown me, as he had already disowned my older sister. A graduate student at Michigan State University, she was a member of SDS and had been arrested several times for antiwar activities. She was also living with a black man, her love life and her politics seamlessly expressing an out-and-out assault on the middle-class American values my parents represented. They'd already lost her, and they were going to make damn sure, for my own good, that they didn't lose me too. To keep me busy when I wasn't on the court, my father got me a job downtown as a stock boy with a novelty wholesaler. Mornings on our way to work, we'd pass the hippies sleeping on the steps of the Arlington Street Church. 'Look at that,' he'd say, pointing at the long hair, bare feet, and dirty clothes. 'If they want to live like dogs we ought to treat 'em like dogs, we ought to round 'em up and shoot 'em. How can they do this to their parents?'

That summer Jeff let his hair grow long, partly to overthrow 'the system', but mostly just to imitate his older brother, who, as I recall, was a rock musician and a poet. Jeff's relation to the counterculture (drugs included) was like his relation to basketball: it seemed to be based entirely in pleasure. To him it was, like everything else, just a trip, just what he was into. In the eyes of others, though, his ponytail meant only rebellion. To his teachers and his friends' parents, mine especially, he became a dangerous, subversive influence. It takes a certain effort of imagination now to appreciate the political valence dress and appearance had in those days. The sign with respect to hair and clothing hadn't yet so promiscuously separated from the signified. Of course, what started as a political statement expressing radical disaffection from the status quo became in no time nothing but a fashion statement that almost everyone was making no matter what the politics. By 1975, even my father wore bell-bottoms, grew longer sideburns, and let his hair inch dangerously down a little over his ears. By 1979, in Skokie, Illinois, the adolescent neo-Nazis – who demonstrated for the right to march through Jewish neighborhoods in which many Holocaust survivors lived – all had long hair and scruffy beards, berets and earrings. They could have been refugees from Woodstock, except that instead of a red fist on their T-shirts they had swastikas, their earrings sporting German crosses instead of emblems of peace and love. In the late sixties, however, dress, appearance, music, and drug of preference defined you quite precisely in relation to the status quo, politically as well as culturally. So much so that, during the summer of 1969, shortly before his trial for conspiracy at the Chicago Democratic Convention, Abbie Hoffman could write, 'I want to be tried not because I support the National Liberation Front – which I do – but because I have long hair. Not because I support the Black Liberation Movement, but because I smoke dope.' As Godfrey Hodgson remarks, Hoffman 'was not saying that long hair and marijuana were more important to him than radical politics. He was saying that they were, to him, inseparable.'

10

Early in the summer, the basketball coach, Don Slavin, asked me to round up a few other players who might still be in town to participate in a clinic for grade school coaches that he and some other high school coaches were running out in Lexington. I went with Jeff, Dale Clark, and I forget who else – there were five of us in all from our team, and some thirty or forty kids from other schools. We all sat together on one bank of stands, the coaches, some seventy or eighty of them, on another. Coach Slavin made some introductory remarks. Then he asked for volunteers to illustrate some particular play or exercise. Jeff was the first kid to jump down out of the stands. This must have been the first time Coach Slavin had seen Jeff since the spring. His jaw dropped when he saw Jeff's ponytail and red headband. 'This is boy's basketball,' he said with mock sincerity. 'The girls don't meet till next week.' Some of the players giggled. The coaches were all dead silent. Jeff didn't realize at first that he was being told to leave. He just stood there, stone-faced, waiting for the coach's instructions. 'Go on,' the coach shouted after a moment, 'go on, get out of here. You're no longer on the team.'

In his defense, let me say that Coach Slavin was a decent man, all things considered. Unlike most of the coaches I had had by then, he was too irritable to be a tyrant. He saw himself less as a Vince Lombardi 'molder of character' than as an undeserving and long-suffering victim of the inadequacies of the adolescent players he was stuck with. During games or practices, he never chewed us out about our failures and mistakes. He never ranted or abused us. Like a despairing husband with a wife he knows he can neither change nor live without, he'd stroke his close-cropped head in exasperation, pleading with us, whining, for God's sake, get back on defense, don't rush your shots, look for the open man. . . . Harried irritability was about as close as he ever got to joy or passion. His dedication to coaching was a function not of an overwhelming desire to win but rather of a fear of losing, of humiliation. Not to be embarrassed by us was his sole ambition. To play poorly, of course, was one thing. To act badly, to show him up before his colleagues, was unforgivable.

I sat there in mortified silence as Jeff walked out of the gym. I was appalled and outraged, yet I knew that if I did the right thing by walking out or speaking up on his behalf I'd be thrown off the team as well. Even later, when the coach pulled me aside to ask what in the world was I thinking of, how could I bring Jeff here and embarrass him like that, embarrass the team, the school, I didn't respond, afraid of what he'd do. I knew that by my silence I had taken sides, and that it was the wrong side. And I felt ashamed.

Jeff, on the other hand, didn't seem to mind. 'What a trip,' was all he said when we met him later at the car. 'What a trip,' as if what happened was

11

just what happened, something to contemplate with fascination or amusement. 'Don't let him get away with this,' I said, now angrier than ever, wanting him at least to stand up for himself since I was too afraid to. 'He has no right to kick you off the team, it's unfair.' But he just said to cool it, basketball just wasn't his thing anymore, coach did him a favor. I was amazed, admiring, and horrified at how easily Jeff could shrug it off, as if it were a superficial inconvenience. Basketball was inextricably part of who I was. Not to be a member of the team was as unthinkable as not to be a member of my family. The claim of both on my identity was so extreme that life without either would have been a moonwalk, weightless and insubstantial.

Still, I was too ashamed of what the incident revealed in me to let it go. That evening, after telling my parents what had happened, I surprised myself by saying I was going to quit the team. They must have known I wasn't serious because, normally, whenever I would announce an intention to do something they flatly disapproved of, my father would bang his fist down on the table and yell, 'Hell you are,' and that would be the end of that. But this time he just shook his head, sorry for me, it almost seemed, as if he knew my self-righteous indignation was a pitiful face-saving compensation for my spinelessness. 'Poor Jeff,' he said, when I finished ranting, 'he just can't find himself.'

Around midnight or so that night, Jeff rapped on my window. 'How 'bout a walk?' Well, if I couldn't give up basketball for him, at least I could break curfew, so I snuck out, and we went up to Cory Hill Park at the top of Summit Avenue. For a while we sat in silence on the small hillside overlooking the city. I wanted to apologise for being such a coward. 'Jeff, ah, about today . . . ,' I started to say, when he interrupted: 'Hey, Al' (he was holding out a joint), 'let's celebrate, man, I'm free.' I'd never smoked dope before. I was a little scared of it, if truth be told. Like all my friends, I ridiculed our elders for believing that marijuana was the first step on the slippery slope that led to heroin, but secretly I half-believed it. I was, moreover, leery of anything, beer included, that might interfere with basketball or jeopardize my standing on the team. But despite my trepidations, I said, Sure, yeah, far out, for Jeff it seemed, was offering me redemption, a chance to make amends, to stand up with him, take his side for once. As I took that first long toke I felt giddy with the risk of it, with doing something I knew would enrage my parents (not to mention what the coach would think); I felt courageous, even principled, like the kind of person I should've been that afternoon.

'Jeff,' I said after a few minutes, 'my dad says your problem is you just can't find yourself.'

'Your dad's a wise man, Al. A guru. I've looked everywhere for me. I just don't seem to turn up.'

'You ought to put out a missing persons.'

'Yeah, maybe.' After a moment he added, 'What do you think I'm doing, wherever I am?'

'Who knows. Balling a chick?'

'Who knows.' Then he laughed. 'Hey, maybe my real self really is an extra large.'

'No wonder he ditched you.'

'Hope he isn't into basketball,' he said.

'Why not?'

'Cause I got his jockstrap.'

We laughed and laughed. I don't think I'd ever laughed with such sheer abandon. The city lay before us in a dense chaotic maze of glimmering lights. Sirens crossed and crisscrossed on the edge of hearing, one now fading away as another now came on, making my being there with Jeff more pleasurable for the continual reminder of what I had escaped. It was as if the sirens were a citywide parental system of surveillance, sounding an ineffectual all points alert that another kid had slipped through its net of warnings, its constraints and hassles – 'Because I said so, that's why'; 'Under my roof, you do what I say'; 'You walk through a field of shit, you're gonna smell like shit.' Another kid had slipped through and entered a forbidden place where there was nothing to live up to, or try for, and therefore nothing to fail at, no one to disappoint.

I was only visiting that forbidden place, though, whereas Jeff, it seemed, was settling in for good. As we started back down Summit Avenue, I was already worrying about how to get back into the house without waking my parents, their imagined fury already closing in around me, sobering me up, bringing me back to the sullen law-and-order earth where I knew all along I had to live. Jeff, on the other hand, was singing in a raspy twang, his head thrown back:

Then take me disappearin' through the smoke rings of my mind
Down the foggy ruins of time, far past the frozen leaves
The haunted, frightened trees out to the windy beach
Far from the twisted reach of crazy sorrow.

Yes, to dance beneath the diamond sky with one hand wavin' free
Silhouetted by the sea, circled by the circus sands
With all memory and fate driven deep beneath the waves
Let me forget about today until tomorrow.

How freely Jeff seemed to come and go. He didn't need to sneak around, as I did, to find what little freedom he could behind his mother's back. He had no curfew, no constraints, it seemed, of any kind. Out of my own

13

dissatisfaction, I imagined that his mother gave her blessing to whatever he did or desired. She let him go his own way happily, guiltlessly, without judgment or resistance. Under the chafing pressure of my father's love, I couldn't recognize back then the almost orphaned loneliness implicit in his apparent equanimity, the 'crazy sorrow' that gave a less than peaceful tinge to his idea of freedom. In this, I think, Jeff was typical of many of the citizens of Woodstock Nation.

'Mr Tambourine Man' was, in fact, the anthem of the Aquarian Age. For the younger baby boomers, those who came of age in the late sixties and early seventies, that song marked the decisive turn away from radical politics to an almost exclusive preoccupation with states of consciousness. Though many rationalized this inward turn by claiming that all politics was personal, that you had to liberate the mind first before you could liberate society, the emphasis was nonetheless entirely on the self's interiority. That rationale, moreover, enabled many kids to justify, on political grounds, what they were doing for purely personal reasons. Now it was possible to get high, go to rock concerts, and 'ball' to your heart's content and think you were doing your heroic part to overthrow 'the system'.

But the quasi-Eastern fascination with altered states of consciousness, with visionary dreams, with less restrictive, less 'bourgeois' attitudes towards sex, love, and material possessions in general, wasn't merely self-indulgent, at least not in any conventional sense. This inward turn wasn't motivated by a rejection of societal norms felt to be too repressive, in the name of robust and uninhibited expression, so much as by a wholesale rejection of ways of being in the world that made one vulnerable to pain and loss. What we all craved, in varying degrees, wasn't freedom, exactly, but a sense of belonging freed from the crazy sorrows, restrictions, and ambivalences of the flawed and contentious suburbs we had come from. We desired to replace our particular identities as individuals, as members of a certain family, class, race, ethnicity, country, and religion, with a transcendent self above and beyond the messy particularities of time and place. We wanted to believe that what you truly were you shared with others. What made them strangers to you, and you to them, your personal history and theirs, your ordinary consciousness with its unique and unrepeatable lore of memory and desire, was really nothing but an inauthentic, because culturally constructed, froth upon a sea of universal being that made us all just one. And if we were all one, if everyone embodied that single human essence equally, then we didn't need to cling to those we loved. And not clinging meant we couldn't hurt, betray, or disappoint each other. What the counterculture offered in effect was not the liberation of feeling, but a collective stoical retreat from all those habits of feeling, thought, and social affiliation that held us hostage to a world that we could not control.

Like ancient Stoicism, the philosophy of free love purged of Western possessiveness and guilt promised a state of mind in which, as Charles Taylor describes the Stoic philosophy of Seneca, 'the soul no longer touched by accidents of fortune is like the upper part of the universe, which rides serenely above the tempest-filled lower air.'

Michael Lang, Woodstock's executive producer, had a similar vision of enlightenment while tripping on acid a year or so before the festival. Lang claims, in fact, that the idea for such a festival originated with this vision of an ideal nation, pictured as a many-tiered structure that is part wedding cake, part magic mountain, and part high-rise shopping mall:

> The first tier was the store with all the paraphernalia, nice karma, peaceful music. The second floor would have subtle changes, the sound and the texture maybe. The walls would begin to lose their shape, items that had a substantial feel would feel different on the next level. Everything would begin to shed its former skin as you climbed higher and higher. As you became accustomed to one experience, you'd want to seek the next. And by the time you got to the top, you were, in fact, free. Nirvana. A floating feeling and sounds, sensations, tastes – all free. A total environment. A nation away from war and racism, where drugs were easily accessible. With rock music and toys everywhere you turned.

The fascinating thing about this vision is the way it combines so many contradictory elements, blending together the traditional image of the spiritual quest as a mountain climb (think of Dante's *Purgatorio*, Donne's 'Second Anniversary', or the allegorical mountain climb in part five of *The Waste Land*) with rank commercialism (the head shop on the first tier 'with all the paraphernalia, nice karma, peaceful music'); political idealism with psychological regression ('A nation away from war and racism, where drugs were easily accessible . . . rock music and toys everywhere you turned'). The higher you go into this spiritual emporium the less distinct everything becomes. Just as 'items' – the mercantile connotations are probably not accidental – shed their skin and dissolve into an indefinite haze, so your own identity (with all its imperfection and ambivalence) dissolves into pure, disembodied feelings, sensations, a floating sentient fetal-like amorphousness. If there's no war or racism in such a nation that's because there's no history, which is to say, no people, no individuals with differing and therefore possibly conflicting interests, needs, aspirations.

Yet to reach that Edenic toy store of effortless fulfillment you have to climb. Implicit in the image of an upward quest (even if it's on an escalator) is the recognition of some degree of effort, struggle, even self-denial.

For those who took it to its logical extreme, the ideal of free love, peace, and harmony through sexual liberation, drugs, and rock music proved every bit as rigorous and severe in its demands as even the most ascetic practices. Some years later, I remember Jeff excoriating himself for feeling jealous at a party when he looked up while 'balling' a girl he didn't know and saw the girl he'd come with 'balling' another guy. Jealousy may be, as he believed, 'a bourgeois fiction', but we were products of the bourgeoisie, and it took terrific effort to extirpate its values and assumptions from the mind. In the same paradoxical way that the doctrine of predestination enabled the New England Puritan to call upon almost super-human reserves of will and ingenuity in meeting the challenges of the New World, the guilt-free ethic of the Aquarian Age produced extraordinary guilt in those who tried to live by it. Perhaps the flower children were nowhere more American than in the puritanical anxiety with which they went about cleansing their hearts and souls of their own past, in the merciless demands they imposed upon themselves to get beyond a culture of demand, self-denial, and guilt.

In saying all of this I don't mean to bash the sixties. Nor do I want to make a virtue of my own deficiencies and claim or imply that my hesitation to follow Jeff into the world he was beginning to enter proceeded from any sort of strength of character, from a capacity to deal unflinchingly with what he and many like him seemed eager to escape. At the time, I saw the counterculture only as a sexual and psychedelic paradise I yearned to enter with hormonally driven desperation, but was simply too afraid to, attached as I still was to my father's love, to the ordinary, angst-ridden, ambivalent relations that nonetheless, with bracing clarity as well as pain, reminded me of who I was. If the euphoria and freedom Jeff pursued turned out to be self-destructive in certain ways, my fear of that freedom and euphoria, if not so self-destructive, was certainly less fun.

However naïve or deluded, however much it was, for many, just a flimsy cloak for other darker things, there's still much to admire in the counterculture's vision of a more cooperative, less acquisitive, less ego-centered way of living in the world. To realize that an understandable disaffection with the status quo, with ordinary life at a particular time and place, became for many of the young a disaffection with life itself, with life as it could be lived by anyone at any time, is not to deny the validity of such countercultural ideals as benevolence and generosity, openness and trust. For all their impracticality, these ideals still serve as an important measure of the possibilities of being, which life now, as we ordinarily live it, has perhaps too easily forgotten or suppressed.

\* \* \*

Much to my surprise, my father didn't threaten to disown me, didn't rant and rave, when I told him Jeff and I were going to go to Woodstock. By that point in the summer, he was too worried about me to make much of a scene, afraid perhaps that if he put his foot down he might lose me as he had my sister. I still dutifully went to work each day. I still played ball in various summer leagues in the evening. I worked hard studying for my SATs so I could get into a Division III school (meaning academically challenging) where I'd have a chance of playing college ball. But I did all this in silent protest, asserting my independence by doing glumly, sulkily, all that he demanded of me. By withdrawing from him, I rebelled against his power even as I submitted to it. Whenever I was home, I stayed in my room and read or studied or listened to the records Jeff would lend me. Late at night, I was also sneaking out with Jeff to Cory Hill Park, where we'd get high and talk and sing. Despite the mainstream's warnings of the evils of dope, I was still no less committed to my various ambitions. Without diminishing my obsessive drive, the dope provided a marvelous relief from it, a temporary space in which I could just be, just enjoy myself with no thought of winning or losing anyone's approval. It was on one of these nights that Jeff told me that his brother had scored a couple of extra tickets to the festival and that Jeff and I could have them. I imagined a festival full of Jeffs, of kids like him, free spirits getting high, balling, dancing to the music we loved. It would be the adolescent version of the party that all of my childhood friends had gotten to go to, a festival of kids from broken homes. Now it would be my chance to go.

'What about basketball?' my father pleaded. 'School? College?'

'What about them?'

'Once you're up there with those hippies, that'll be the end of that. Believe me. I'm telling you, you won't come back.'

He seemed more sad than angry, his sadness a mixture of befuddlement and defeat, as if his only hope now of holding on to me were to let me go. In me at that moment I think he saw the ironic fruits of a grimly virtuous existence, of a lifetime of denial and self-sacrifice in the name of making life easier for his children. I don't think my father ever held a job he loved, or ever expected to. Whether he was serving as the foreman in his father's slaughterhouse, or running the belt manufacturing business that his brother owned, or, as now in 1969, a salesman in the men's department of Saks, work always and only meant the antithesis of pleasure, self-expression, and fulfillment – the flower child's holy trinity. Work was what you did for money, and money in turn was what you laid away, first for your children's education, and then for your retirement so you wouldn't have to be dependent on your children in your old age. This dedication to our welfare he never lorded over us. The dedication was simply how a man, a father, was supposed to live. If you expected a medal for acting like a mensch, then you were definitely not a mensch. What he expected of me was respect, by which he meant conformity to how a man should live.

I don't think either of us realized that afternoon, as we sat across the kitchen table from each other, that my generation's utopian expectations of a life of play and freedom were created by the very material comforts his generation worked so hard to give us. When I think now of all the pleasures we regarded as our birthright, the moral constraints and inhibitions that had defined his life, and that we cast aside, to quote Philip Larkin, like 'an outdated combine harvester', I imagine that there must have been some element of envy in his disapproval. He may have glimpsed in our rebellion an image of freedom he secretly desired. And glimpsing this, he may have felt like an unacknowledged and embittered Moses, watching his children crossing over to the very promised land to which he'd led them, but was too old himself to enter.

Max Yasgur's farm did seem like the promised land to me and Jeff when we arrived that Thursday afternoon, a day before the festival officially began. Jeff's brother told us Woodstock would be one gigantic communal happening, so we didn't need to bring anything with us but a sleeping bag. When we got to the camp grounds, he and his girl friend set up their tent, laid a few joints on us, then sent us on our way.

By that time there were already some sixty thousand kids scattered across the fifty-acre farm. We found our way to an area called Hog Farm, named after a commune based in New Mexico, a hundred of whose members had been flown in by the festival organizers to help with crowd control. These were career hippies, the freaks of the freaks, wholly dedicated to communal living and enlightenment through dope, acid, and organic food. They had set up a free kitchen for those who had come without money, and various first-aid tents for kids on bad trips or overdoses. There was a small stage there as well, where lesser-known groups performed for those who couldn't get to the main concert. Everyone was very friendly in a cosmic, dreamy sort of way, some of the men in dresses, pajama bottoms, buckskin trousers, vests patched together with pieces of the American flag, the women in long peasant skirts, some in Day-Glo halter tops, some bare-breasted, with naked babies in their arms. One guy in a white toga, sandals, and top hat walked past us saying over and over to himself, as if it were a mantra, 'I peak therefore I freak.'

As a city kid who'd never had so much as an outing in the country, I was utterly taken by the pastoral setting, the wide fields sloping into one another, the green ponds, the patches of woods, and the blue sky overhead as deep and clear as it must have looked on the first day of creation. There were no police, no authorities, it seemed, of any kind. Here we could do openly with no fear of reprisal what we had grown accustomed to doing late at night behind locked doors. Wherever we happened to be, at any time, without anxiety or circumspection, whenever we wanted, we could get high or ball our brains out if the opportunity arose. Truly, it seemed, we had entered a new world that stood on its head the values and mores of the old one. Maybe my father was right. Maybe I wouldn't return.

Late in the day, we came upon a large pond where thirty or so kids were skinny-dipping. Without hesitation, Jeff took his clothes off and joined them. I hung back. I was deeply self-conscious about my own body. Even to take a shower in the privacy of my own bathroom I had to overcome some degree of inhibition. And even though my girlfriend and I had been sleeping together for several months by then, the lovemaking was always furtive and shy, our bodies only glimpsed in the flurry of passion while before and after we were careful to keep close enough to one another so as not to get a panoramic view. What I found remarkable and chastening was how relaxed everybody seemed to be. They were physical in their naked-ness without being sexual at all. They played and cavorted as if they all had clothes on. Wading in among them in my cutoff jeans, because I was the only one still partially dressed, I felt as if I were the only one exposed. It seemed that everyone but me had somehow figured out a way to reattach the apple to the tree of knowledge. What I wanted to do more than any-thing was gawk at all the pretty girls, but gawking would have violated the Edenic code of innocence. Instead, while Jeff cavorted with the others as if they were his lifelong friends, I looked casually ahead at no one in par-ticular at the same time that I desperately tried perfecting my peripheral vision, ogling breasts and asses out of the corners of my eyes.

I was so distracted by the naked flesh around me that I didn't realize that Jeff was gone. Eventually I found him back at Hog Farm among a bunch of people doing yoga. As I approached, a man was talking to him and the other kids. He was older than most everybody else, maybe in his mid-thirties, and he had short hair. I realize now he must have been a cop, one of the hundred or so brought in by the festival security team in case things at any point got out of control. In keeping with the atmosphere of benevolence and trust, the cops didn't carry guns, and aside from being older and having shorter hair, in their jeans and T-shirts they looked and acted like the rest of us. Anyway, by the time I got there, the guy was claiming to have just returned from a Zen monastery where he'd been ini-tiated into a highly secret form of meditation, but in honor of Woodstock, he'd let us in on it. It was designed, he said, to bring Nirvana to your very bowels. More likely, though, it was the other way around, for what he proceeded to do was squat down like a sumo wrestler, and with his hands held before him palm to palm, his head bowed reverently, his eyes closed, he began to fart, fart with a capital F. I mean, these weren't just ordinary farts, these were long frank inexhaustible belches he seemed able to release at will, in different keys and registers as he moved from one position to another, now waddling like a duck with his ass cocked first to this side, then to that; now swiveling his hips like a belly dancer, swiveling and grinding them, his arms held over his head while his head bobbed side to side, forward and back. The Zen of farting. I have to admit that for a while I was taken in. Only someone with almost mystical control over his body could vigorously fart at will the way he did. Then I remembered what we'd all been eating at the free kitchen (it wasn't called Hog Farm for nothing) – beans and brown rice. By then everyone was flatulent enough for true enlightenment. Most people think the haze hovering over Yasgur's farm that weekend was marijuana smoke, but me, I'm not so sure. In any event, Jeff exclaimed 'Oh wow!' and began to imitate the man, and the others followed suit till there were maybe fifteen or twenty new initiates all letting it rip as they squatted and rose and waddled, lifting up first this cheek, then the other, in a kind of Animal House imitation of tai chi.

When the group broke up the cop put his arm around one of the more 'enlightened' girls. 'Your spirit's just amazing,' he was telling her as they went off together.

'What a gas, no pun intended,' I chuckled as Jeff and I walked away.

'What do you mean?' There was no amusement or irony in Jeff's face or voice.

'Jeff, you can't be serious. That guy was putting you on.'

Jeff put his two hands on my shoulders. 'Al,' he said, looking straight into my eyes in that obsessively earnest way of his, 'you gotta be more trusting, man, you're too uptight, it's like you're stuck in prison, in solitary, and there's all this beautiful shit going on outside, and you're all alone pretending there isn't 'cause you can't be part of it.'

Though there was more to my skeptical detachment than mere inhibition, Jeff was right. I was uptight and too distrustful, more so than usual, to my surprise, at the very time when I should have let myself relax into what was happening around me. Among so many people, all of whom, in Joni Mitchell's words, were content to be 'a cog in something turning', I had to insist on being different, better, shrewder. If, in the name of that communal embrace, they were happy to be duplicates of one another, to be heads, freaks, hippies, transparent in their openness and gullibility, I would by my very watchfulness become opaque, mysterious, dense with complexity, too streetwise and knowing to be the butt of anybody's joke. While this standoffishness prevented me from being duped, it also cheated me to some extent of the experience itself, of living it more deeply, or more richly. I was an American middle-class adolescent version of the speaker in Baudelaire's 'Le Jeu', who sees the limited being of the whores and gamblers crowded around the gaming table, but at the same time recognizes in their obsessions and addictions a fiercer hold on life than he possesses, his own compulsion not to live but to stand back and observe in the nonbeing of detached superiority.

A little later, we settled down for the night on a hillside we had entirely to ourselves. Despite the night sky busy with shooting stars, the balmy weather, the one last joint we smoked, nothing could break the chill our differences had placed between us. We lay there in awkward silence, Jeff probably thinking that if Woodstock was a trial of my allegiance to the new enlightenment, then clearly I had failed it.

To give me one last chance, he asked me how much money I had, and if I'd split it with him.

'What happened to your money?' I asked. He said he'd given all of it to some Hog Farm freaks.

'And what are you gonna do with the money I give you?' Suddenly I sounded just like my father.

'Probably donate that, too,' he said. 'They need the bread. Anyway,' he added, shrugging, 'it's only money.'

Only money. Only basketball. The records, the books he gave me and never wanted back. Everything abandoned with the same shrug of easy acceptance, which only now began to seem forlorn and fatalistic, not liberated in the least. Jeff hated things, I think, because things broke, things meant anxiety and worry. If you gave them away before they were taken from you, then you at least had some control, however self-destructive, over what might happen. But there was also a social dimension to this personal asceticism, for the less you had to lose, the less chance there'd be of being envied and disliked, and the easier it was to get along with others. If you had no material advantages, nothing to distinguish you from others, to set you apart from then, then nothing could be expected of you. And you had therefore nothing to live up to, which is to say, nothing to fall short of. Implicit in the communal harmony Jeff desired was an idealized family in which the collective is the happily married parents, and the individual is the child, and the love between them is unconditional, instinctive, and unlosable, falling like sunlight impartially on everyone, no matter who they are or what they do.

But for me, what I found most difficult to accept, what I instinctively resisted, was the ideal of passivity (what Jeff would have called receptivity) at the heart of this vision of the good life, the anti-perfectionist perfectionism that required its followers to abandon any upward notion

21

of self-refinement, any notion that by dint of conscious effort, practice, dedication, you could redefine the limits of what was possible, which in art and sport defines the truly excellent.

* * *

As odd as it may sound, it was my athletic training and not just my inhibition that made me balk at the counterculture's invitation to seize the day. All through grade school and high school, day in, day out, in the gym and on the playground, with simple-minded dedication (or was it obsession?), I had given myself over to the discipline of learning how to play the game of basketball. I had learned to dribble, shoot, and pass with either hand. I had learned how to study my opponents and adapt my own play to their strengths and weaknesses. By subordinating myself to the discipline the game required, I'd become a better, more imaginative, more versatile player. And that convinced me I was capable of overcoming other sorts of obstacles, on and off the court. And while I eventually ran up against the limits of my physical abilities – no amount of practice would make me six foot four – that freedom to resist my limitations, to change myself, and its collateral gifts of concentration and sheer undiscourageable doggedness, would serve me later when the poems I was writing challenged my mental and imaginative powers.

Jeff had what seemed to me a horizontal vision of the good life, in which pleasure, spontaneity, and freedom were not in hock, as they were for me, to discipline and sacrifice. It may be that my more vertical understanding of the good life is partly a fancier version of the upward mobility that drove my father's life, a transference to the realms of art and sport of the competitive virtues of the marketplace. Now, twenty-five years later, with children of my own, I can admit what I would have been too eager to deny back then: that I am, for good or ill, my father's son, a child of the American bourgeoisie. So too, of course, was Jeff. The new self he struggled to become was no less dependent on the values and practices of the culture he was struggling to define himself against. Yet when I think about the kind of life I wish for my own children, I can't help but think my vision of the good life, despite the many ways it unconsciously participates in the less than ideal features of American life, is simply better than the one Jeff pursued, better because it gives a more potentially inclusive image of human flourishing.

As we fell asleep under the stars, Jeff was no doubt lost in his contemplation of the night sky, wholly absorbed by the amazing light show overhead. I was thinking that when I got back to Boston I'd have to make up for the time away from basketball by doubling my evening workouts.

22

I was awakened at dawn when someone stepping over me accidentally kicked me in the head. The hillside we had entirely to ourselves when we closed our eyes was now entirely covered with people, shoulder to shoulder. They had come all through the night. Rumor was that Route 17, the main road that led into the festival, was backed up for miles. Ignoring the fields the organizers had reserved as parking lots, the kids grew tired of being stuck in traffic and just abandoned their cars right there on the road and hiked the last few miles to the farm. Word had also gotten around that the festival would now be open to the public, a free concert. This decision was made less out of generosity than out of fear that if the organizers tried to collect money from the kids who had already crashed the gate they'd have a riot on their hands. The festival designed to accommodate maybe a quarter of a million people now had twice that many. Imagine a subway car at rush hour jammed wall to wall with people, then project that human density over a fifty-acre farm, and you have some idea of what the crowd was like.

By dawn on Friday the weather was already hot and sultry, the air so humid it was like breathing someone else's spit. The humidity also seemed to bring out the mosquitoes. I should add here that I am and always have been a kind of human No Pest Strip. If no one else among the five hundred thousand people at the festival seemed bothered by the bugs, that's because all the bugs were buzzing greedily around me, a Woodstock Nation of them feasting at the free kitchen my body had become.

I wasn't surprised to find that Jeff had split. Anyway, with my eyes nearly swollen shut from the mosquito bites I hardly cared. I spent the better part of Friday standing in lines. I waited for several hours to use a portable toilet only to find the stench so blindingly repulsive that I couldn't enter. Eventually I found a relatively open field where other people were shitting and pissing, and being by that time more desperate than shy, I happily joined them. Then for several more hours I waited in line at the Hog Farm free kitchen for a plate of something that looked and tasted as if it came from someone else's stomach. It was after five then. The concert had begun. I was too tired and uncomfortable to work my way into the massive audience. Besides, I had to keep on moving to keep from getting bitten by the bugs. As night fell, and the rains came, in a crowded field among tents and plastic huts I lay down utterly miserable, soaking wet, and exhausted.

Just after dawn on Saturday, I saw the person I would come to think of as the queen of Woodstock, the living enactment of the euphoric ideal that would lead Jeff over the years from commune to commune, drug to drug to detox center, till he disappeared entirely from the lives of all his old friends. I saw a naked woman in a mud hole in the middle of a path. Kneeling in the mud, she was slowly, almost ritualistically, taking handfuls of the thick brown muck and smearing it down all over every inch of her, her hair, her face, her neck, breasts, hips, and belly, a darker caking of it on her crotch. When she had covered herself completely, looking less like a woman dreaming of herself as mud than like mud dreaming of itself as a woman, she began to dance among the people swarming past her, her hips swaying, her arms held over her head, her eyes closed, her dark smiling face all dreamy inaccessibility. Now and again, a man or woman would dance in front of her for a moment or two and then pass on, while she, oblivious, continued dancing, her trance unbreakable, the queen of Woodstock Nation floating blissfully free beyond 'the twisted reach of crazy sorrow', beyond her name, her past, her family, even her sex, forgetting in the moment all the gravities that held her to the world beyond the moment.

Later that morning I caught a ride on a departing garbage truck. I rode on the running board, clinging to the door handle as the truck lurched precariously forward on a shoulder of the dirt road that led out to the highway, halting and inching onward against the jubilant stream of people still arriving, everybody smiling and flashing peace signs to me as I started back in the direction of my anxious father.

from

*Mixed Company*
(1996)

## The Letter

The letter said you had to speak to me.
*Please, if you love me, Alan, hurry. Please.*

I read it and reread it, running down
the big stone steps into the underground,

and every time, as in an anagram,
the letters rearranged themselves again

as new words canceling the ones before:
*Come or don't come I really couldn't care.*

*I never meant to hurt you like I did . . .*
*I never hurt you. There's nothing to forgive . . .*

The letter virulent with changing moods,
now cross, now pleading, accusing and accused,

seemed to infect each place I hurried through:
the slippery concrete of the vestibule,

the long low tunnel, and the turnstiles where
nobody waited to collect my fare,

nobody on the platform either, far
and near no sound within that mineral air,

nothing around me but a fever of clues
of what it was you wanted me to do.

O mother, my Eurydice in reverse,
was it the white line I was meant to cross?

To hear within its Thou Shalt Not a 'Shall'
and follow you into a lower hell?

The page went blank. Below me now I saw
barbed wire running where the third rail was,

and in the sharp script of its angry weaving,
suspended in the loops and snares, the playthings

of forgotten life, dismembered dolls,
the frayed tip of a rubber knife, a wheel,

the tiny shatterings of cups and saucers,
and other things worn back into mere matter,

their glitter indecipherable except
as the star burst of some brief interest,

the barbed discarded relics of a wanting
they all intensified by disappointing.

As if they could be words, and those words yours,
obscuring what they substituted for,

each leading to a darker one beyond
the bleak lights of the platform, I jumped down

and there at last among them crawled and read,
burning with comprehension as I bled.

The pain was good, the pain exhilarated,
the pain was understanding, now perfected.

Cauled in my own blood, mute and lame and free
of everything obstructing you from me,

I saw your face above me leaning down.
*There's nothing here for you,* you said, *go home.*

*It's for your own good, child, believe me,* and
I vanished, waking as you turned around.

## My Mother and a Few Friends

My mother and a few friends at a table,
talking, smoking, entirely at ease
because alone at last. I'm somewhere there
among them, but too small to matter, made
invisible, it seems, by everything
I don't yet know. The men are gone, as usual,
where I couldn't say for certain, though
it's easy to imagine them as having
drifted away together, groggy with eating,
to go on talking money, money, meaning
who got taken for a fucking, and by whom,
and for how much. But now, if heard at all,
their voices reach us from so faraway
that nothing of what they say's discernible
beyond the half-consoling, half-dyspeptic
rhythm of the adages they answer
one another with – 'Business is business' . . . 'You got
to speculate if you want to accumulate . . .'
'The only thing that grows in your hand is your pecker . . .'

Who else beside my mother's at the table?
B.Z., Pearl, Gissy, Dot, or Ann?
And anyway to know this and be able
then to say with confidence they're close
to the beginning of more than forty years
of just such afternoons, before this one
dies, or that one moves away, or sickens,
is not to make it any easier
to look beyond my having known them now
for so long otherwise, as middle-aged,
as old, and see them as I saw them then.

Even my mother's vague, being so young,
her face so much a restless shadowy
idea of being young, and stylish:
the blonde hair tinted blonder, teased and sprayed,
the just-so hint of rouge, the glistening lips,
her features (like the features of her friends)
meticulously shaped to the desire

29

for the thoroughly prescribed, thoroughly
extraordinary future all her own.

By then, of course, enough of their real future
(though only enough perhaps) would have arrived
to make that general postwar thrilled
expectancy as difficult to be
believed in as abandoned. By then, too,
even among each other, there would have been
the usual envies, petty grievances,
slights and disappointments. I know. I know.
And yet despite this (even perhaps because
of this as well), the picture of them there,
and of myself among them, is a picture
somehow haunted still by happiness:
happiness too peculiar to themselves, though,
too elusive being so much theirs,
so near, so ordinary.

                      The women keep
on talking, and I watch and watch, and all
I make out clearly is the cigarette
now one and now another hand is waving
into strands of smoke that tangle and run
together whenever anybody speaks:
I watch until it seems the voices are
themselves that swirling gauze, secretive, communal,
hung there to say, whatever else the words
were saying, we are this, and they are that.

## Wife: Labor

The pain inhaled you,
and you groaned it out in no voice
I had ever heard before, a voice
anterior to yours, archaic, fierce,
from so far deep within you
I could hear the rock vein, mineral
mother-lode
the aboriginal
first freak of pulse was
ripped from
once and now returned to
for the force it needed.
And as the head crowned,
as the blood-crowned
head emerged it was
your body only now that spoke,
your face unrecognizable,
wrenched tight as rope,
hands twisting in the sheets,
and what it started to
say then in anguish,
blood, excrement, it
finished saying later
when the nipple
between your fingers brushed
the baby's cheek so deftly
that she turned to suck:
you would have died to save her
if you had to, and if she died
you would have raged,
you would have grieved and lived.

## Isabel

When you were three days old, your mother sang to you.
Cradling you at last, holding to your mouth the tube
of oxygen you couldn't breathe without, for the first time
in a voice made tentative with gladness still too new to trust,
more brave than beautiful, she sang your name, sang
over you the quavering song of every syllable she wanted
to prolong, to keep repeating till she was certain
the astonished welcome of it had settled in your ear
so deeply that you would hear her singing even later
when the singing stopped and you were taken from her.

Despite the panting lungs, the bruised arms, the tubes and wires,
how calm you seemed then (even the doctor noticed).
Watching you both, I knew as I've known little else
that years from now, alone, in company, waking
or edging into sleep, when over you there falls
as if from nowhere, too suddenly to be explained,
a joyous sense of being wanted here in the world, –

not knowing that you are, you'll be remembering this.

## Night Terrors

Whose voice is it in mine when the child cries,
terrified in sleep, and half asleep myself I'm there
beside him saying, shh, now easy, shh,

whose voice – too intimate with all the ways
of solace to be merely mine; so prodigal
in desiring to give, yet so exact in giving

that even before I reach the little bed,
before I touch him, as I do anyway,
already he is breathing quietly again.

Is it my mother's voice in mine, the memory
no memory at all but just the vocal trace,
sheer bodily sensation on the lips and tongue,

of what I may have heard once in the pre-
remembering of infancy – heard once and then
forgot entirely till it was wakened by the cry,

brought back, as if from exile, by the child's cry, –
here to the father's voice, where the son again
can ask the mother, and the mother, too, the son –

Why has it taken you so long to come?

## Single Mother

### 1.

I can recognize the tiny subterfuge: how the mother,
giving her child exactly what he's asked for, has escaped him
without him knowing that she has: higher, he said, higher,
until she hardly has to push the swing now and can
safely close her eyes, and doze, and for a moment
      not be anybody's mother.

The price of that leisure, though, is to be startled
when he cries, to feel ashamed, too, by the sweetness
the cry disperses. So that she seems almost to wish
her voice, full of more solace than he cries for now,
could deepen his distress and so intensify for him
      the pleasure of her taking it away.


### 2.

Most mornings he's up at five, she says. By nine, bored, cranky,
he wants to go somewhere but won't let her dress him, wants to eat
but not anything she offers. Then he starts crying for daddy, he wants
his daddy. That's when the weariness turns suddenly to rage,
her body one white knuckle of rage, and she has to get him quick
out of the house, somewhere where just the presence of another
mother will protect them both from what she otherwise might do.


### 3.

His first and last assumption. His given,
as enveloping as air, and like air
to his breathing, unrecognized

as needed, being always there.
Moody weather he wakes up to,
atmosphere perpetually charged

with emerging and dispersing
fronts and pressures that are themselves
the indecipherable effects

of earlier weather in another sky
he can't see yet is helpless
not to read for any omen of himself.

Beyond which only the outer space
of not her goes on and on.
Everywhere beyond her what

her distractions, daydreams, brief
luxuries of blank attention
hint at, and make him have to cry

sometimes to call her back from:
what his dark bedroom hints at
when she leaves it, too tired

not to, though he calls and cries,
too obviously glad, yes glad
for a short while at least,

to leave him finally in the nowhere
of her hurrying away,
fleeing momentarily away

for once to where no gravity
at all can keep her from forgetting
her relief can only mean his terror.


4.

The moment my son and I arrived she started talking,
at swing first, then at sandbox, while the boys played,

talking incessantly in a low drawl of exhaustion
one could easily mistake for a drugged calm.

As if her voice just couldn't wake, it seemed to sleepwalk
through a single sentence, incontinent with revelation,

about how they have no choice now but to put up
living with her mother till she can find a job,

because her ex-husband, among other things
couldn't stand the mess the boy made when he ate,

and how his tantrums scare her, he can really lose it,
especially in public, which is so humiliating,

what are you supposed to do in front of all those people?
and does mine love Bambi as much as hers?

and did I ever notice that the mother's always killed off
in those movies, or locked up, or somehow gotten

out of the way before the child does anything
at all remarkable to show he's worthy

of growing up into a prince, or star, or daddy? . . .
Despite the drab sweatsuit, the squall of unkempt hair,

the deep fatigue around the eyes and mouth, there was
about her a stubborn loveliness I can't pretend

I didn't notice whenever she would, yawning, arch
her torso toward me just a little, or when her long hands

seemed to parry, in slow arabesques and curliques,
the thrusts of what she couldn't help herself from saying.

Wouldn't it be less than honest not to say I listened,
or appeared to listen, not out of sympathy alone?

that listening was the coin I paid to take her in
more freely, to revel in my own way in the little

resonance of possibility our being there
with children made it completely safe for me to feel?

And if she suspected this and went on talking
to me anyway, as if I were the dreamed-of mother

or friend whose ear she always had the pleasure of, –
so desperate to be listened to, to be coddled with listening,

that she'd indulge my eye, so she could have herself
this ersatz intimacy – wasn't it, all in all, a fair transaction?

Not children anymore, don't we at times use each other,
pay each other one way or another for the pleasures

that, however briefly, bring us to the child's
exhilaration that the mother can't not hear or come?

The way she heard when the boy called and immediately
hurried over to see what it was he wanted.

And the way, too, suddenly like a girl, she swung herself
as if no weight restrained her onto the monkey bar,

to hang there upside down above him, laughing,
swinging, holding her hands out so her fingertips

would graze his when he leaped up to grab her,
leaped and missed. And even though he started to cry,

though he was crying now, she howled like a monkey
for a moment longer, just for the pleasure of it.


5.

The night-light diffuses paler darkness through the dark
around him, soothing for now, from his features, all fevers

of appetite; all spasms of raw will ease,
effaced in such excess of peace there's little

left of him but dream sounds, mews, sighs, vexing
the silence so faintly they seem to deepen it.

Here, at least, is patience, inexhaustible
so long as there's nothing else to worry over

but the covers she has to put back gently again,
and again, across him when he turns or shifts.

Here now his breathing is the tide she drifts on
toward sleep at last, but slowly, not yielding yet,

though sleep is all she's yearned for all day long.
She holds it off, delays it, to prolong

this present moment of a mothering
that isn't withering her, or marring him.

*Pleasure*

Ever obliging, faithful, good parents that they are,
when he's happiest, in his happy bed, his wife against him,
they call to him, his tutelary spirits of a moment
hidden now inside his pleasure, as his pleasure's underground.
They call, and the rapt eclipse, the mutual gasp and cry,
is suddenly the golden bough leading him back down stairs,
a child again, to the doorway where his mother stumbles,
yelling something, with her arms held like a shield before her
as his father swings, – just that, and nothing else beyond it,
no before, no after, and no terror either but the terror
of remembering that he was thrilled, not terrified at all,
as if they knew what would please him before he did himself,
tightening all along the coil of what he didn't know
was there, of what they hid from him so he would feel
only the sheer pleasure of its fierce release.
It was their first, their clearest lesson in fulfillment.
Ever after only the tantalizing substitutes, the sulks
and silences, the spectral pantomimes, that left him
more expectant, hungry, dreaming the ever more vivid
dream of what they wouldn't do, withheld, he realizes now,
so he'd always want that pleasure, know how incomparable it was.
Here, where he's happiest, with his wife beside him, his hand
no heavier than breath along her arm and shoulder, they bring
him back to the original event because they love him, flesh
of their flesh, they want him to have everything they had.

*Lethe*

You called me to come see the bees. Come out of the house
you called once, in a bad time, when we were lost to each other,
blurred by habitual regard, disgruntled and aloof
though not from injuries, but from a hoarded sense
of being injured, precious so long as vague, vague
        so long as silent.

By the marigolds you planted they were all hovering,
hundreds of bees, it seemed, like bright flecks of the lavish
blossoms they were drawn to, each long stalk tipping over
under the pressure as they clung together, crowded and swarmed
the way Vergil says the souls do by the waters
        in Elysium:

even there among the blessed groves, the lush green
of bodiless pleasure, weightless now, unstrictured,
free, they swarm to drink oblivion and again put on
the body's weight. I leaned down close to look, to see
what you saw, and as I did, unconsciously you rested
        one hand on my shoulder,

in an old way, dormant for how long? Time, unresting time,
beautiful and perverse, how suddenly it could lift us
clear of our own shade to a luminous attention
it just as suddenly extinguished, as the bees moved on,
the shade, now, darker for that brief respite. *Poor souls*, Aeneas asks,
        *how can they crave our daylight so?*

## Soul

If, as they always claim upon returning,
there's only radiance there, near death, and in
that radiance the brighter densities of all
their own beloved dead come out to greet them,
and they themselves now bodiless, rinsed clean
of eye or ear, are able to perceive them;
if it's the after-image of the body
only, the thinning yet still sentient mist
of who they were, that keeps them only far
enough away from what they brighten toward
to know themselves as its auroral edge; –
Why then do they return?

                    Couldn't it instead
be the body that rejoices there?
that radiance the body's radiance
of being only just aware enough
as body to know it is itself the star-
flung anonymity it's on the verge of
when the suddenly too quiet quiet
startles the soul awake, and soul comes rushing,
calling and rushing like a fearful and
ferocious mother to her only child?

## The Friend

Fidgeting with the beer she doesn't drink,
one finger picking at the softening label,
careful to peel one corner, then the other
free, without it tearing, she tells me
she much prefers pain to embarrassment,
and everything about the whole affair –
that Karl had been both her and her husband's oldest,
closest friend, that they had coddled him
through two failed marriages, and when their own
faltered, that he'd become her confidant,
and then, of course, her lover – everything now
but his betrayal's so degradingly
predictable in a suburban pot-
boiler sort of way that the betrayal
itself seems almost redemptive, almost a gift.

Joe never suspected anything, too busy
making up excuses for the book
he couldn't get around to writing – he needed
better software, the apartment was too noisy,
her presence distracted him too much, her absence
put too much pressure on him to produce . . .
just once in all those years of working, putting
her own ambitions off so he could bask
fretfully in the glow of his potential,
just once she would have liked to say, please, darling,
take all your clothes off, stand before the mirror,
and ask yourself, for once, now really, does this
look like the center of the universe?

And yet it took those long first intimate talks
with Karl to realize just how lonely she'd
become, how angry, how dissatisfied.
Yet less for anything he might have said
than for the way he simply listened to her,
he had a woman's way of listening,
sympathetic, compassionate, engrossed,
with none of that distrustful, briney-with-judgment
air of insecurity she'd grown

accustomed to. And it was woman-like,
as well, the way he utterly forgave
his ex-wives for their flaws, mistakes, deceptions,
yet seemed so merciless about his own;
the way he showed such deft, exquisite feeling
for the messily extenuating, nearly
indecipherable relatedness
of how things happen, so that the more he told,
the more she in response would tell until
she found herself confiding things she thought
she'd never ever say to anyone.

By then, going to bed had come to seem
merely the next inevitable step
to a yet deeper conversation. Well,

o.k., she was a fool not to have seen
where that one led. She should have known Karl,
being a man, like any man, once she
was free, would hem and haw the feeblest things,
straight from the Soaps, about him needing time,
he's so confused, he cares so much about her . . .
and on and on until you didn't need
a psychic to foretell the clichés those clichés
were leading to, cold feet, cold shower, cold storage.

If that were all, though, she could write him off
as a delusion born of the disease
her marriage was, humiliating, yes,
and sad too, yet not really that disastrous.
Even the sex, though good, was mostly just
the novelty of being wanted once again.
Why she might even feel now that she should thank him
for having helped her get out of the marriage.
If that were all. If not for the betrayal.

No, the betrayal changed him, made him, she
admits, more interesting because more vexing.
Or maybe it's the other way around.
In any event, the puzzle of it isn't
that he and Joe throughout the whole affair
would often get together behind her back

(so Joe would tell her later, to punish her
when he found out what they had done to him),
or that they met here at this bar, at this
particular table where she and Karl would go
to talk, where she and I talk now. Or that
Karl was the one who would arrange the meetings,
who'd try to draw Joe out. Or even that
the two of them discussed her. No, it was
what he would tell Joe when Joe began to fear
that he was losing her: night in, night out,
sometimes before he'd see her, sometimes
afterward, from this table to her bed,
from her bed to this table, he would go
to Joe and tell him, Joe, don't be a fool,
whatever you have to do to keep her, do.

And looking down now at her hands, as if
they're hardly hers as they begin to shred
the label into small and smaller pieces,
she wants to know if I was aware of this,
since Karl was my friend too, and still is?
And I say, no, not really. Which is true,
I wasn't, not of that, at any rate,
although I thought that I knew everything
there was to know about the two of them.
And suddenly now it shames me to remember
my pleasure in those intimate conversations,
how it delighted me to hear Karl say
there's no one else whom I can tell this to
but you. Delighted me he needed my
approval, my acceptance. I realize
I'd have forgiven him almost anything,
even this betrayal, and almost feel
betrayed as well that he would keep it from me.

So for a moment I'm not sure who she means
when she asks, mostly to herself, it seems, –
more troubled than enraged, more curious
than troubled, even cool in the obses-
siveness of the pursuit of what eludes her –
could anyone's attentions be so absorbed,
so voluptuously taken by the moment,

that he himself believes the only friend
he's ever really had is the one he happens
at any given moment to be with?
A friendship junkie? I ask, half-joking,
and she says yes, now looking straight at me,
a friendship junkie, hooked on the sensation
of being thought the perfect friend, the thrill,
too, maybe keener for the coming crash,
the crazy uncontrollable momentum
carrying him along toward certain trouble,
happily not knowing when or where or how.

Or maybe she's got it all wrong, and as she says so
sweeps the tiny pieces off the table.
Maybe he was only all along
so in control that he could make detachment
look and feel like love, like sympathy;
maybe everything, right from the start,
even years ago when she and Joe
were adequately married, if not happily so,
maybe everything even then had been
methodically foreseen, arranged and plotted, –
if that's the case, then was the thrill he sought
the thrill of knowing she believed she'd found
in him the perfect friend, the perfect lover,
while all he'd ever found in her was just
the best available ingredient
for another story that had nothing
at all to do with her, so he could bring
that story where? to what? these very questions
she's unable now to answer or not ask?

She shrugs, and smiles, and says all right, now you talk:
what do you think he wanted? And as if
she knew already whatever I might say
but only asked so she could hear me say it,
she's looking past me, bored, when I part guess
and part confess that what he might have wanted,
what might have thrilled him most of all, would be
to know somehow she'd come back here with me,
to talk to me all night about him, talk
all night about him to another friend,

another man who, since he is a man,
must have his own designs upon her. Wouldn't
that be the ultimate kick, I ask, to know this?
But she says nothing, holding her bottle up,
waving it to catch the waiter's eye.
She hasn't listened to a word I've said.

## In the Land of the Inheritance

*In those days there was no king in Israel: every man
did what was right in his own eyes.*

— Judges 19–21


A foreigner and his ass and concubine
were huddling in the square as night came on;

around them, veil on veil of dust that hoof
and staff and sandal could only disturb enough

to show how calmly it was sifting down
into a darkening sabbath of its own.

Surely here, he thought, among the Benjamites
someone would ask him in to spend the night,

and he, a holy man, the lord's anointed,
chosen among the chosen. But while he waited,

merchants and tradesmen, young and old alike,
all hurried by without a word or look

to their own dwellings as if he wasn't there,
and only the ache from having come so far,

his sharpening hunger and the night's chill
told him he was not invisible.

His concubine kept silent, her veiled head bowed,
since it was her fault they were stranded now:

Hadn't she tried to run away from him
back to her father's house in Bethlehem,

and when he came to get her, her father said,
'My son, my son,' and gave him wine and bread,

and blessed him, and then told the girl, 'Go home.'
So now he glowered at her. 'See what you've done,

impious woman, see what your unclean ways
have brought us to,' he was about to say

when an old man who pitied their distress
said, 'Peace be to you, friend, come to my house,

I'll give you food for hunger, wine for thirst.
Come to my house, I'll care for all your wants.'

Now as they ate and drank, as their hearts grew merry,
the townsmen gathered together in a fury

outside the old man's house and beat his door,
and yelled, 'Old man, give us the sojourner

that we may know him, give him to us now.'
The old man pleaded, 'Leave the man alone,

my brethren, he is a holy man, a priest,
all he has asked for is a place to rest.

Here is my virgin daughter, here is his wife,
take them instead and do what to your sight

seems good to you, but do no wickedness
against the Levite whom the Lord has blessed.'

But now like locusts ravaging a field
the men surged forward, shouting, and would not yield

until the Levite, knowing what he owed
the hospitality his host bestowed,

pushed out his wife alone and shut the door.
One by one all night they ravished her.

She ate dirt all night, and when they were through
they left her in a befouling solitude

of being known to each and every man,
exposed and filthy, utterly smeared with sin.

And he, whatever struggle he endured,
hearing her call him at the door he barred,

whatever turbulence of rage and shame
swept through his heart as she called out his name

before the other voices carried hers away,
subsided now as he began to pray,

grew faint, and fainter, until he realized
the Lord was with him, and the Lord was wise.

So even when he discovered her at dawn,
and she just lay there, though he told her, 'Come,

let us be going,' he knew it had to be
the Lord who guided this iniquity,

who in His marvelous power understood
everything that had happened (and now would),

who steeled within him such a righteous calm
as he laid her on his ass and brought her home –

the Lord's hand holding his that held the knife
and sharpened it and took it to his wife,

and delicately with a jeweler's care
severed limb from joint, and joint from ligature.

All day he worked, he drew the blade down deeper
into the far recess of every chamber

as if each membrane were another veil
he'd cast aside and find the soul revealed.

The soul, however, above the gaping flesh
was hovering, now free of all distress,

serene because she saw what he was doing,
could see as fact the aim he was pursuing –

how all of her, obedient to his will,
would go throughout the land of Israel,

a piece to every tribe, which they'd receive
and be astonished at what it could mean, –

could see them all from Beersheba to Dan
come to the Lord at Mizpah as one man,

four hundred thousand strong, and all now ask
how this abomination came to pass, –

could see them raise their swords together high,
vowing the men of Gibeah would have to die.

So rapt in the unskeining of her vision
of every consequence of his decision,

she almost didn't hear the Lord call, 'Come
my Daughter, it's time to come to me, come home.'

But she refused, and as his 'Daughter, Daughter,'
closed in now echoing everywhere about her,

she let go and dissolved and all He found
was mute dust sifting to the bloody ground,

back to the flesh her husband would disperse
throughout the land of his inheritance.

## Manufacturing

Up in the billboard, over old South Station,
the Captain, all wide grin and ruddy cheek,
held up a golden shot of Cutty Sark
high as the skyline where the sunset spread
a gold fan from the twig-like spars and rigging
of a departing clipper ship. Above
the picture the dull haze of a real sun rose,
dragging the day up with it. Seven o'clock.
The agitated horns, brakes, fingers, and catcalls
down below me were already merging
and channeling everybody on to warehouse,
factory, department store and office.

My father and uncle talking over all the goods
to be received that day, the goods delivered,
their two reflections in the window floating
like blurry ghosts within the Captain's grin,
their voices raised a little above the soft
erratic humming of the big machines,
the riveters and pressers, warming, rousing:
The Century order, did it get out last night?
And had the buckles come from Personal?
Who'd go do Jaffey? Who'd diddle Abramowitz
and Saperstein? Those cocksucking sons of bitches,
cut their balls off if they fuck with us . . .

How automatically at any provocation
I can aim the words at anybody now,
woman or man, the reverberating
angry this, not that, in 'pussy', 'cocksucker',
'fuckhead', hammered down so far inside me
it's almost too securely there to feel.
But I was thirteen then, and for the first
time old enough to have my father say
these things in front of me, which must have meant
I was a man now too, I listened (blushing,
ashamed of blushing) for clues of what it was
I had become, or was supposed to be:

51

It did and didn't have to do with bodies,
being a man, it wasn't fixed in bodies,
but somehow passed between them, going to
by being taken from, ever departing,
ever arriving, unstoppable as money,
and moving in a limited supply
it seemed to follow where the money went.
Being a man was something that you did
to other men, which meant a woman
was what other men became when you would do them.
Either you gave a fucking, or you took one,
did or were done to, it was simple as that.

Somebody shouted from beyond the office
that Tony had passed out in the can again.
'The lush, the no good lush,' my uncle said,
'get him the fuck out of here for good, will ya.'
The stall door swung back, scrawled with giant cocks,
tits, asses and cunts, beyond which in the shadows
my father was gently wrestling with the man,
trying to hold him steady while his free hand
shimmied the tangled shorts and trousers up
over the knees and hips, and even got
the shirt tucked in, the pants zipped deftly enough
for Tony not to notice, though he did.

Even then I knew they'd fire him,
and that it wasn't gratitude at all
that made the man weep inconsolably,
his head bowed, nodding, as my father led him
to the elevator, still with his arm around him,
patting his shoulder, easing him through the door.
I knew the tenderness that somewhere else
could possibly have been a lover's or a father's
could here be only an efficient way
to minimize the trouble. And yet it seemed
somehow my father was too adept at it,
too skillful, not to feel it in some way.

And feeling it not to need to pull back,
to separate himself from what the rest
of him was doing, which was why, I think,

52

his face throughout was blank, expressionless,
like the faces of the presidents on the bills
he handed Tony as the door slid shut.
The men fast at the riveters and pressers
and the long row of women at the Singers
were oil now even more than men or women,
mute oil in the loud revving of the place,
a blur of hands on automatic pilot,
slipping leather through the pumping needles,

under the thrusting rods, the furious hammers,
the nearly invisible whirring of the blades.
'Come on now, Al, it's time,' my father said,
and the Captain seemed to grin a little wider,
as if his pleasure there at the end of his
unending day grew freer, more disencumbered,
because he saw me at the start of mine,
under my father's arm, his soft voice broken
against the noise into an unfollowable tune
of favors and petty cash, and how much ass
he had to kiss to get me this, and I
should be a man now and not disappoint him.

## The Basement

How many years, decades, since I'd even thought of Gary
when my mother told me on the phone the other night,
in passing, that he'd been thrown in jail for kiting checks,
and that this on top of all the other heartache Gary's mother
had from him, the busted marriage, the drug problems,
had sent her to an early grave. But it wasn't Gary's mother
I thought of as I listened but the basement where we spent
most of our afternoons one summer, the two of us and Helen.
Helen, the only German Jew I knew, who'd come after the war
from someplace else, not Germany (though no one told me where),
to live with them, to be his nanny. He called her Zumzing
because she hardly spoke except to ask, every so often,
can I get you zumzing, Gary, you vant zumzing now?
and whether he wanted anything or not he'd answer,
get me zumzing Zumzing, and laugh, so I'd laugh too.
Helen, though, unmindful of the teasing, or inured to it,
which made it easier to do, would hover over Gary,
her readiness to please him unassailable, yet strangely dour,
joyless, like someone on indefinite probation for some crime
nothing she could ever do could quite make up for.

Whenever he'd ask, she'd get the bottle Gary said
wasn't a bottle but a big cigar. Though eight years old,
he'd nuzzle against her, 'smoking', gazing at nothing,
Helen stroking his hair, reminding him, Vee don't tell Mama,
dis just our secret, vee don't tell your mama now,
at which he'd pause, grinning, saying Vee dis, vee dat,
with the cigar held gangster style between his fingers.
It never occurred to me to make fun of him.
He'd look up from the bottle from time to time, and smile,
and seem so certain I'd admire him for this, I couldn't not.
It was as if in going down into the basement
he'd gone beyond the reach of how we usually were,
becoming at the same time both older and younger
than he should have been. It thrilled me, being there
with him, all the rules suspended, making new rules up,
the games he'd want to play so like and unlike
the games I knew that to play them was to feel
myself complicit in the secrets he and Helen shared:

Whoever was 'it' would be buried under cushions,
and stay there dead while Helen counted to a hundred.
Then 'it' would roar and rise and hunt the other down,
whipping him back into the pit where he'd be buried.
Or with the cushions Helen would wall in a corner of the basement,
and Gary and I would take turns guarding each other, marching
back and forth before the entrance, a rifle on one shoulder,
until the prisoner watching for the slightest lapse
would storm the gate, all of the cushions tumbling
down around us as we wrestled to the floor.

I remember reading of the children in the camps and ghettos,
how in their stubborn urge for pleasure where there was no pleasure
they'd pretend the horrors they were living through:
the bigger ones who got to be the Germans whipping and beating
the smaller ones who were the Jews, to dig their graves,
stage funerals, line each other up, and through it all,
German and Jew together, they would all be laughing.
During the war, wouldn't Helen have been about the age
that we were then? I wonder now what she was seeing, or
wanted to see as she looked on, waiting until the play
got too rough, as it always would, and one of us would cry
before she'd pull us off each other and, hugging Gary
or hurrying to get him out another bottle, ask
in the same flat tone, Now vee do zumzing else now, jah?

My mother didn't know where Helen was now,
or whether she went on living with the family
after Gary dropped out of high school and moved away.
She said it drove his mother crazy, how she spoiled him rotten.
Did Helen mourn the trouble he got into? Or had she
by the time we knew her had her fill of mourning,
her heart by then concerned with other things, things he
unwittingly provided, Gary never more enslaved
than in the license she made him think was his? Could he
have been her plaything too, as much as she was his,
her puppet of a secret brooding on what couldn't be forgotten,
all of her life from the war on (and she was just a girl then)
a mere reprise, a deafening echo chamber?
                                        And even now
I wonder who's obliging whom when Helen –
after all these years of never being thought of, lost

among the minor people of my personal history –
rises from the dead through small talk to become
my personal link to what I can't imagine.

It almost seems I have my way with her again,
seeing her there in this last scene, down on her knees
surrounded by a chaos of innumerable pieces
of the train set she's saying is like the one she played with
with her papa long ago, an aura of dread and urgency
about her as she hurries to put it all together, working
to keep us down there with her a little longer,
to keep us from going anywhere she wouldn't follow
(did I ever see her leave the house?): all over the basement,
the tracks in curves and straightaways, the signs for Stuttgart,
München, Würzburg, Berlin, the flashing signal lights,
the flagman in the switching yard, black-coated porter at the station,
and beyond it shops, cafés, and houses, a church and school –
the flanged wheels fitted to the tiny rails, and Gary
settled in her lap now, his hands on the black box
easing the levers as she whispers dis one, jah, now dat,
and the cars click forward through that miniature world.
Soon, though, bored, he throws the black box down, and he and I
rampage over everything, stomping and pulling it all apart
while Helen laughs (the only time I ever heard her laugh).

## The Fight
### 1969

The black girl next to me was cheering under her breath
as the two girls, white and black, appeared to freeze

together for a moment with their hands locked
in each other's hair before they toppled over

in a blur of pummeling. Get the Bitch, Dolores,
she was saying, abuse her, eat her up, her faint voice

giddily enraged, yet cautious too, confused,
it almost seemed, uncertain of its own excitement,

as if she'd grown so used to wishing for what she saw
she only half believed she saw it now before her.

Right on, girl, right on, she cheered a little louder,
the voice rousing itself past hesitation or demurral.

And though the rest of us stood there, dumbly looking on,
and would later try hard to range in, cage what we saw

with outrage, stories, rumors of who said what and why,
till we could think it didn't have to do with us,

my friends and I – white friends and black friends –
did any of us at the time make any move to stop it?

Wasn't hers the only voice of what we all were feeling,
and were dismayed to feel, were too well trained to show?

All of us rapt by the tribal solvent of our civil dream,
by the frenzy of slashing nails, ripped blouses, shrieks

and muffled groans; the girls dissolving in the mouth
of rage beyond their names, or sex, or even the history

that carefully prepared them for the dissolution, –
dissolving in the idiot mouth till in the teeth of it

they could only go on tearing at each other, kicking
and scratching even after the teacher intervened.

Old court. Old chain net hanging in frayed links from the rim,
the metal blackboard dented, darker where the ball
for over thirty years has kissed it, the blacktop buckling,
the white lines nearly worn away. Old common ground
where none of the black men warming up before the basket
will answer or even look in my direction when I ask
if I can run too, the chill a mutual understanding,
one of the last we share, letting me join them here,
if nowhere else, by not letting me forget I don't belong.

Old court. Old courtesy, handshake, exchange of names,
in the early days of bussing, between assassinations,
before our quaint welcoming of them had come to seem,
even to ourselves, the haughty overflow of wealth
so thoroughly our own we didn't need to see it.
Old beautiful delusion in those courtly gestures
that everything now beyond our wanting just to play
was out of bounds, and we were free between the white lines
of whatever we assumed we each of us assumed.

Old court, old dream dreamed by the weave, the trap,
the backdoor pass. Old fluid legacy, among the others,
that conjures even now within our bodies and between them
such a useless, such an intimate forgetting, as in the moment
when you get a step on your defender and can tell
exactly by how another man comes at you
where your own man is and, without looking, lob the ball
up in the air so perfectly as he arrives that
in a single motion he can catch and finger roll it in.

Old court. Old dwindling cease fire, with no hope of peace,
that we silently turn away from when the game is over,
hurrying back (as if believing contact meant contagion)
to our separate tribes, to the cleansing fires of what,
despite ourselves, we momentarily forgot:
old lore, old news, old burning certitudes we can't
stoke high or hot enough, yet won't stop ever stoking
until whatever it is we think we are anneals
and toughens into an impenetrable shield.

from

*Covenant*

(1991)

## The Sweepers

Who were they? The writer just calls them 'sweepers', clearing
the streets, leveling a path for the army through the smoldering
debris of ancient houses torched and toppled all about them.
For six days, their heads bowed to the task, as they were told,
nameless, stateless, were they slaves, now serving other masters,
having already learned this lesson, neither saddened nor relieved
that the rooms they served in were now rubble to be pushed aside?
Or that their masters lay there crushed among the stones
and timbers, some of them still wailing, calling out for mercy
as they shoved and turned them over, old hands at going on?
Or were these the masters? the wealthiest? their money,
somehow, having gotten them this far, as yet unharmed?
their fingers blistering as they plied crowbar and boat hook,
dowel and axe, the pain a punishment for the dumb animal
persistence that so easily and thoroughly turned friend and relation,
the whole rich tapestry of customary feeling, law, memory and lore
into mere fill for gullies? – Did they resent the half-dead
for their clumsy fit, their ineffectual resistances,
the ones stuffed head down, legs above the surface
writhing pathetically to get away, like giant insects,
or the ones feet first, their heads above the surface
unable even to flinch as the horses trampled over face and skull?

The writer doesn't say. For a few lines in my Roman history,
for six days and nights, nameless, stateless, ever diligent
they clear the streets, they make the way smooth for Scipio,
who, it is said, was weeping, sunk in thought, as he looked on,
weeping at the fortunes of cities, peoples, empires:
the Assyrians had fallen, and the Medes, and the Persians
after them had fallen, and so too, latest of all,
latest and most brilliant, the Macedonians blotted out,
destroyed, as Ilion had been destroyed, and Priam,
and the people of Priam of the strong ash spear . . .

Here one turns the page, and goes on reading.

## Maison des Jeunes

'Nuit sans étoiles, nuit obscure'
– Baudelaire

After the woman I was visiting had gone in to bed
some nights I would see a woman undress on a balcony.
The long playground below us, which our building fronted,
would already be deserted by everyone but the men
at their game of boules far at the other end. Their pitch,
the only strip of dull light cut in the darkness
made duller by the slow twining of cigar smoke
over and around them, the quiet made more quiet
by the random click of the balls, by the laugh or groan
that would rise for a moment above the constant
murmuring and then fall back.

                                All through the twilight
I would look out toward her building and never know,
for certain, who she was among the countless mothers
on balcony after balcony hanging up and taking down the day's wash.
The same clothes always in different places, a sluggish
eddying of orange and blue, white, pink or olive
blouses, pants, slips, socks and dresses up and down
each bleak façade. Her voice, somewhere among the voices,
would have been calling from time to time down to the playground
loud with children, a mesh of excited cries, shrill bits of singing,
from which each magnetic call, weary or cross, or both,
would pull in one reluctant child, and then another.
When the dark thickened, always the same two remained:
a fat boy dribbling a soccer ball in one place
fluidly from knee to knee to forehead back to knee,
while a friend bicycled around him, veering as close
as he could to swipe the ball away, and always missing,
because the boy, clairvoyant in his own finesse,
would take one half-step back or forward, shift the ball
so tauntingly beyond the other's reach the other,
jittery with hope, would have to go on playing.

                                      Each night
the longer she would keep me waiting, the more unexpected
was her white shirt's fluorescent glow against the dark,

down which her vague hand moved from button, I imagined,
down to button until her shoulders arching back
a little let the loose shirt slip as smoothly as water
down her bare arms. Her dark skin now so merged with darkness
that the sudden black flare of breast was like a gift
the late hour gave and took away, so as to urge from me a more
intense stare that would later make her memory keener than sense.
Maybe her husband was among the men she could have watched
passing in and out of small groups now, to and from their turns,
a bottle drifting languidly from hand to hand; slower
and slower, as though to prolong each other's reverie
of these after hours, postponing each waiting bed,
each getting up tomorrow. Maybe she could have heard
her husband among their voices, the seamy, intimate, male
exchange of secrets they (their scant wages already portioned to their wives)
had earned the right to keep. If only one of them had seen her
she would have been another secret in the smoke-slurred
light of their little freedoms; she would have been in his mind,
later, as he lay down beside his wife.

                    As I lay down,
she was the woman I would need to wake, those nights,
waking my friend. Hers, the darkness that would open up for me,
draw me down deeper, and never deep enough. Beyond me, always,
the promise of her unseeable face, the mild dreamy argot
of her moaning what could have almost been a name.

## Mud Dancing
*– Woodstock, 1969*


Anonymous as steam, in the steam teased
from the mud-hole at the field's edge
where we were gathered, the unhallowed dead,

the herded up, the poured out like water,
grew curious about us – naked as they were
once, our numbers so like theirs,

and the air, too, a familiar newsreel
dusk of rain all afternoon.
It could almost have been themselves

they saw, except that we were dancing
knee deep in mud, in the muddy
gestures of their degradation,

unpoliced and under no one's orders
but the wiry twang and thump
we danced to, sang to, yowling

on all fours, hooting on backs and bellies,
smearing black lather over our own,
each other's face, arms, hip

and crotch till we were sexless, placeless,
the whole damp mesh of who we were that made us
strangers to each other, the shalts and shalt

nots of you and me, mine and not yours,
cast off easily as clothing
into the blurred shapes of a single fluency.

Was this some new phase of their affliction?
The effect of yet some new device –
to make them go on dreaming, even now,

some version of themselves so long accustomed
to their torment that they confused
torment with exaltation, mud with light?

*Frau History*, they asked, *is this the final*
*reaving of what we loved well, that we should*
*swarm now in the steam over the indistinguishable*

*garments scattered everywhere in piles, that*
*we should need, even now, to sort through them,*
*to try to lift in our vaporous hands*

*the immovable rough granite*
*of this sleeve or collar, that vest,*
*those sandals, the flimsiest top?*

## Virgil's Descent

Not Moses but another Tantalus –
to have been granted this much, and no more,
to see beyond the stream he'd never cross,

near but no nearer now, on the far shore
those hymning veils impenetrably bright
about the gift he was not chosen for.

His only grace there on that blessed height,
as he turns back, would be another chance
to climb down like a body from the light

slowly enough to see its radiance
shine dim and dimmer in the rising eyes
he sinks past, past their lightening penitence,

down through the fire that scorches till he dies
of being unsinged in that weightless flesh
each step leads further now from Paradise.

Upward forever, the flayed gluttons, whores,
killers and con men to their just reward,
all jostling by him in a holy mesh,

each soul a syllable within the Word
he'll study, and repeat, and never master
century after century . . . Now they deboard:

the naked cargo of a new disaster,
women and children, Gypsy, Slav and Jew,
their charred flesh smoking out of every boxcar,

eerily in the steam they wade out through,
down the long platform, shivering, half-afraid
they're not arriving but returning to.

They hurry off, they scramble in the prayed-
for dark, away from the wandering aura where,
never more hopeless, never less assuaged,

he sings, he sings about the burning sphere
of love not meant for them, whose burning fueled
another kind of transport straight to here.

The more he sings, the more the song seems cruel,
and more mysterious – the merciful
bright manna now an ash of syllables

he can't not sing, the more they fade and swirl
endlessly in and out of one another
over the floor of that vast terminal

the way birds at a sudden shot will scatter
to far trees, and still farther, as if they
could hear the sharp blast echoing forever,

and nowhere could be far enough away.

## Night Watch

He pauses where the road crests,
and somewhere deep in the woods
a dog rouses: the faint
howling so far up back
behind the trees it seems
to come unplaceably
from all directions, more
the nimbus of a sound,
he thinks, than sound,
what the stars would be
as voices as they slant down
the steep night into the massing
thicker night of trees
below him, each one howling
its colossal earth-dwarfing
fire over light-years
of light-years to this
speck-like brushing in his ear.

Who was it? What was his name?
More than a thousand miles from here
and over thirty years ago,
who was the boy who told him –
one night behind the school,
in the alley where the older boys
like cavemen huddled round a fire
were playing cards, by matchlight –
that everything anybody
ever said on earth had to
rise through the night sky
and say itself forever
to the stars, and past them;
every wisecrack, or lie,
even the soft slap of card
on pavement, the clinking coins,
the terse nova of each struck match,
fading forever but never faded
as they rose; and that some day
he would invent a radio

so powerful it would gather up
his voice last week, last year,
the first word he ever spoke,
and transmit it back
through the crackling
interstellar airwaves?

Even now up past the Dog Star
he would be saying
that boy's name as they parted,
as he always did, as if
he would always say it,
as if each time didn't bring him
closer to the year
or two, or more, when he would
say it for the last time
here on earth – saying it
again beyond the Dog Star,
the North Star, Bear and Archer
in a voice he wouldn't recognize
if he heard it now.

*The Lesson*

For a long time afterward
all I could think of
was the one time
he took me: the slow
ride back, him saying,
see, like this,
his fingers claw-like
against the wheel,
like this, with the seams,
let's see you do it,
now snap it down hard
this way, that's right,
that's the fuckyknuckle.
And he smiled then as if
he saw ahead of him
all the things I'd do
with what he showed me.
I remember thinking that
if people on the street
had seen the pebbly
gold sheen of the car
among the ordinary
traffic, if they had seen
him talking, smiling
when I held my hand up
claw-like, just like this,
they would have thought
he was a proud father,
I was a lucky son.
How would I ever say
to anyone who he was?

I was ten that summer,
and I loved Rich
with a keen aimlessness
I couldn't name, or hide,
or not let draw me
to the playground every day
to wait for him, to wait

there, restless and sullen,
with a few friends
who were nothing more
to me but glum
reminders of what I was
without him, what I
couldn't be till he arrived.
It didn't matter that
I knew he came just
after one each day –
I still tried
to convince myself
each moment he didn't show
was just proof he wouldn't.
I tried to work myself up
into utter hopelessness
so I would feel – when the gold
Sting Ray came round the corner –
how suddenly waiting
could not be waiting now,
not having having.

And what I had, then,
was an almost holy
feeling of unworthiness
that he would come
at all: Rich
all the more mysterious
for looking just like
anybody's father
in a brown suit, tie
he never loosened.

How's it hanging?
he'd ask us from the center
of the chrome-lined golden
nimbus we couldn't keep
from touching, drawing
our hands over the sloped
sides, the grooves and channels,
and the sleek wedging
where the headlights hid.

The whole car radiant
with everywhere he'd been,
everything he'd done.

How's it hanging, boys?
he'd ask, and tap
the wheel, jiggle the stick,
the engine revving
gently, not so gently,
to remind us of all
the other things
he could be doing.

Were we Little Leaguers?
Did we want to learn
a cool pitch no one
else knew how to throw?
It was a combination
screwball/knuckleball
he called a fuckyknuckle.
And he would teach it
to each one of us. Promise.
And we'd never lose.

So how could we not
want to please him
when he'd ask if
anyone could tell him
what pussy was,
slit, gash, hole?
What made hair
grow on our palms?
What did it mean to
dip the wick? To bugger?
Bang? Ball?

            And what
seemed to please him
most was how we giggled.
Giggled because we knew
the words were power
without quite knowing

what the power's for.
He liked to see us struggle
not to look away;
he'd smile, then,
without derision, awkwardly,
his eyes just a little
bit averted, as if
our high-pitched ignorant
unease aroused some
unease in himself,
as if the words so
casually uttered in his
deep voice, then repeated
skittishly in ours,
had brought us both
to the edge of some
forbidden place, or,
rather, to two
forbidden places – his place
for us, ours for him.

Then the rides started.
Each day, he'd want to know
who's hanging longest?
and before we could answer
he'd pick just one of us.
Each day it wasn't me
I'd watch them vanish
round the corner and
imagine as they shot down
avenue and boulevard
how the speed would be
its own green light
through all the intricate
traffic-guiding grammar
of signs and signals, the two
of them a bright blur
past the marveling neighbors,
past the houses, schools,
out beyond the city
to a blessed grove
of going even faster.

When they returned, the boy
would never say
what happened, where they went.
Aloof now, troubled,
it seemed, by being
back among us, he would move
in what I took to be
an otherworldly charm,
a secrecy
of having been beyond
anything we knew
or had words for,
but Rich's words. That's why,
I thought, nothing
was ever said, and why
from then on he didn't
stammer, as we did,
or blush, or stand there
scolded when Rich chose
another boy, and still
another to go off with him.

Till, Hey, stop pulling your pud
and get in, he said
one day, and suddenly
all the complex multi-
colored gauges were
before me, their arrows
trembling up
eagerly for the speed
Rich held back as we
crawled down side street
onto side street.
Where were we going?

Hey, had I seen
the Dick Stick?
From the glove compartment
he pulled out a rubber
penis that fit
over the stick.
And shifting from first

to second, back to
first again, he
stroked the grotesque
veiny sides of it,
tickled the big head
and chuckled to see me
chuckle nervously.
If I didn't want to
touch it, I didn't
have to, I didn't
have to worry, nothing
was going to happen.

Now we were somewhere
among deserted buildings,
back behind a warehouse,
at a loading dock
where the yellow grease-
smeared tongues of
fork lifts stuck out
over the edge above us.
Leaning closer, he said
it's weird, isn't it?,
he said it slowly
too earnestly,
with so much more fear
than I was feeling
that I began to feel
really afraid.

Then he reached over,
his hand batted my arm
playfully, his fingers
now a language in which
the words make sense
but not sentences,
weirder for being
almost understood.
It's ok, I thought,
this is ok, this one
hand tickling my side,
just like my father's –

('horseplay' my father called it) –
so I squirmed and
giggled, giggled louder
to make it horseplay,
to make myself not
feel the unintelligible
other hand get
my belt unbuckled,
unzip my fly and
with one finger
lift the underwear's
elastic band and let it
snap back, lift and
snap it back again
and again while he only
let himself lean
close enough to peek
in bashfully, peek,
then look away,
as if to show someone
outside the car that
nothing had happened,
see, everything's fine.

A boy is nowhere
else more boy-like
than in the way he
imagines being a man.
My boyhood ended
there, that day, with nothing
else to take its place.
Now I had no name
for what I was.
To try to think it,
say it, was to look
down some vast avenue,
through an infinity
of red lights
and not know any
word for green.

The last day we saw him,
someone's mother was
coming up the street,
coming quickly, yelling
you boys, you
get away, go home,
get away from him.
And he was out of the car,
standing before her
(it was the first time
we'd ever seen him
outside the car),
head bowed, hardly taller
than we were, stammering
I didn't do. . . . I didn't . . .
She'd have him locked up,
did he understand,
locked up with all
the other psychos
if he ever ever
came near her boy again.
Her finger jerking
in his face while
everything about him –
the glassy eyes, the hands
held out in pleading,
and the mouth trembling,
wordless – said back
it wasn't fair, said it
like any boy punished
unfairly, as if her accusation
made him innocent, and this
I would come to think
was what he must have
wanted all along.

At that time, though,
all I saw was the back wheels
of the Sting Ray skidding
as it shrieked away,
the mother stalking after,
still pointing, yelling;

all I could feel
was my throwing hand,
the fingers flexing claw-like
and still more claw-like,
till I got it right.

## Love Poem

*'If the last day were come, we shouldn't think so much about the separation of friends or the blighted prospects of individuals . . .'*
– from *Cape Cod*, Thoreau

Our first warm morning,
and all over the yard
insects had hatched
invisibly and were swarming
up from the grass, innumerable
in a blurred light of wings,
dizzying helixes of rising
through leaf-shadow and sun,
and all so slowly, all
hovering now or dipping
down before they fanned out
higher and wider, as if
to dawdle in that first
moment of their being
suddenly in air, half
resisting their own urge
upward so as to feel
the pull of it more keenly.

Imagine at the appointed hour
what it will be like:
earth's old bonds broken,
all the nations of all time
whirling in a haze, and you
and I lost to each other in that
joyously forgetful going;
imagine our flesh –
the jury-rigged and sweat-stained
ark we danced before,
danced hard as we could
in sun and leaf-shadow –
scoured to mere radiance! Odd,
and not comforting at all,
to think that even to wonder
where you were in that

79

multitude, to want to
loiter there with you
a little while
among the shadows, would be
too great a gravity
ever to rise against.

## In the Kingdom of Pleasure

Unwitting accomplice in the scheme of law
she thought to violate, man-set as it was,
and, here, inconsequential as the sun
at midnight, drought at flood-time –
when she heard a baby in the tall reeds
at the river's brink, she was nobody's
daughter, subject of no rule
but the one his need for her established
as she knelt down to quell his crying
with a little tune just seeing him there
had taught her how to hum.

                 Now as then,
it is the same tune, timelessly in time,
your mother hums as she kneels down
beside your little barge of foam,
smiling to see you smile when she wrings
out from the sponge a ragged string
of water over the chest and belly,
the dimpled loins, the bud so far
from flowering, and the foot slick
as a fish your hand tries to hold up
till it slips back splashing
with such mild turbulence that she laughs,
and you laugh to see her laugh.

Here now, as it was then, it is still
so many years before the blood's smeared
over doorposts, before the Nile clots
with the first-born, and the women
wailing, wailing throughout the city;
here now again is the kingdom of pleasure,
where they are safe still, mother and child,
from the chartered rod of the Fathers,
and where a father can still pray, Lord,
Jealous Chooser, Devouring Law, keep
away from them, just keep away.

## Separation of the Waters

In his voice I hear the first day
      of the waters,
before the spirit moved, brooding,
      over the face of them,

before the firmament appearing
      in the wake of His Word
divided upper water from lower water,
      heaven from earth,

on the second day. Here in his voice
      the first day
once again refuses the command
      to be the second,

vowel and phoneme all awash, inchoate
      in a jubilant babble
I lean over the crib to watch, that goes on
      after he sees me,

after I say the name he hears as nonsense
      the way the waters heard,
so entangled in the waters, whelmed
      in the jubilant eddy

of such complete embracing they couldn't
      have known themselves
as water, when the Lord said,
      'Let the waters part'.

See how as on the shore of speech, lonely
      for him, I call and call.
See how the syllables begin to dampen,
      blur and dissolve back,

close as they can now, toward the far surf
    they were torn from,
from the shore of the sixth day calling
    back to the first.

*Turn*

Speech is the candle here – see the dark made mobile
now about its tongue, the gathering dark of voices
earlier than ours, and others still earlier, voice
ringed on voice out to the first rough filial hue and cry.
Here, we say, I'm here, turn to me now. Who is it speaking
in the circling namelessness? By whose breath is the flame fanned?
Speech is the candle I hold up to see you
and the night bent down to cup us in its giant hand.

## Home Movie

*– for Beth and Russ*

That's your father, she tells us, when he was nice.
Our father with you sleeping in his arms, his first-born,
his month-old daughter, and our mother next to him –
when I was pretty, wasn't I pretty? – her blond hair
banged and glossy, and her bright face keen above
the clean white petals of her blouse's collar,
keen and yet stiff too, smiling for the camera
at the baby she just knows she'll be a sister to,
and at the husband who could be a movie star,
he's such a looker, then out at us, forty years away,
then back again, the whole time smiling, smiling,
eager to seem as happy as she is. She's just nineteen.
Impossible to tell, meanwhile, which part is love
and which part shyness keeps him staring down
at you and never at the camera, his big hand
fussing the blanket back below your chin,
even after she starts teasing, elbowing his side
to make her 'big baby' smile, just once, at us.
Yet there's something sure there too, skilled even,
in the clumsily tender way he holds you out now
like a thing too precious to be held, as if
he knew it made him better-looking, that furtive
half smile harder to resist because withheld so long,
taken back so quickly, which is why he's not surprised
when she laughs at this and kisses him on the cheek;
no, not surprised but boyishly triumphant – to have
won over, so easily, so beautiful a woman.

Their good looks float unsteadily on the scored surface.
Hard, and long, and unimaginable – the way here.
Imagine, though, we were the movie they were watching,
and they knew us, knew who we were, as in a dream,
a bad dream he would not believe – your husband's black skin
like a cruel prank and, crueler, your lighter daughter
sleeping in your lap, your first-born, late child
we have come to celebrate, and, no, that couldn't be
his wife beside you, overweight, sad, everything
inscrutable but her sadness, which he'd misunderstand;

85

and she, too, still a child herself, like any child
would be afraid what her friends would say, her family,
baffled to be in the picture, baffled yet maybe
reassured as well, her hopes not entirely unfounded,
to see how eagerly she lifts the baby out of your arms
because you're tired and should go lie down, and how
you two laugh together, as if you'd done so always,
when she takes the tiny fingers in her finger
and waves them forty years away to where
she's waving your hand in the same finger.
Bitter, and long, and unforeseeable – what changes,
what survives! She holds the small hand toward us
and in a girl's voice, wonderstruck, says she read
somewhere how the skin will darken as the child gets older:
Isn't it lovely how dark it is under the fingernail?

## Purgatory

They are there now on the twilit platform,
all of them glancing at each other
in a tightly strung decorum
it confuses them to know so well.
Like a sleep they can't quite
yield to, or shake,
everything they see –
the broken heating lamp,
the trash bin, benches –
is veiled in a wavering air
of unplaceable reminders.

All they can think to say
are tag ends of phrases,
debris of idioms they repeat
and shrug at helplessly –
*Far Out . . . I wouldn't give*
*two cents . . . My luck . . .*

How odd, too, still to be shifting,
steadying bundles in their arms
for ease, when they're not tired;
still to be stamping their feet,
beating thick-coated arms, breath
steamy, when they aren't cold.
Why must they lean out
over the edge to watch the rails
curve into far-off trees; why want
to see the rails flare, the flare
slide nearer, the train light glimmer
through the branches till it
floats free, drawing the train behind?

It's as if these gestures
were a rumor of some missed
connection that concerns them.
a map they still know
how to follow even after
they've forgotten what a map is.

If we would only think of them
a young girl might come
skipping up the stairs,
vain, foolish, smiling at
no one, humming some silly tune
that's her own affair –
yet they would see her
rising toward them like a flower
from the lower dark
and in the light of her
would know the words
for uncle, friend,
lover, child and parent;
with their own names
suddenly sayable
they would see, beyond,
in answer to her coming,
how the light glides free
of the branches
down the black trough,
closer; just as in answer,
too, they would feel
again the glad weight
of these belongings
heavier in their grasp
as they are drawn now
to the girl, to swarm
around her, gently,
unhurriedly,
certain that where she is
is where the doors will open.

Memory, Memory,
see how they wait there
in the mere occasion
of their looking
everywhere around –
see how they wait for you,
too shy to ask
(even if they knew how),
Is this the right stop?
Am I supposed to be here?

## Covenant

The oldest sister, her two hands on the table,
about to push herself up, stares with grim
determination at the affronting dishes,
waiting, it seems, until the middle sister
finishes her story, so she can clear them away.
Her gaze so tense with purpose she can almost
see germs spawning in the mess of white fish
flaking from the spines, the smear of egg yolk
and the torn rolls disfiguring the china;
as if the meal, the moment it is over,
the meal she made a point of telling them
she shopped for, got up early to prepare,
were now inedible, because uneaten.
It's no great comfort either that her brother
sitting opposite holds up a flared match
over the pipe from which smoke rolls away
across the table like a phantom mold
in and around the open tub of butter,
the gouged block of cream cheese and the coffee cups;
so in a moment when she finally does stand
she'll say again, as always, For love or money
in my mouth I'd never put such filth,
and he'll say, winking at the middle sister,
That's what she said on her honeymoon.

The youngest sister is sitting on the couch
behind the table; her face – sheer disengagement,
toneless and still – appears to hang suspended
beyond the oldest sister's shoulder, far
enough away for no one yet to notice
as her legs cross that the ashtray in her lap
spills ash over the sunflowers of her housedress.
Or that the cigarette between her fingers
sags loosely and is dangling while the hand
lifts like a puppet's on a string of smoke.

Her death is just three months away.

Even though it's summer (otherwise
the brother and middle sister would be home,
in Florida), summer and late morning –
with sunlight only just now catching on
a corner of the window shut behind them,
shut against the smog, the steady traffic
and the panicked blare and drawn-out whining fade
of sirens – the apartment is still quiet,
still cool enough, right now, to keep the body
in the wavering frail zone of what it needs
to be forgotten, so they can sit like this
together, with the older sister's sharp eye
on the wrecked meal, the brother and sister talking:

Listen, she would be saying, listen, Charlie,
her elbows on the table, both hands open,
the body fashioned to the voice's weary
What can you do? What are ya gonna do?
in answer to some story of a cousin's
sudden illness (And he was my age, just
like that one day he's shaving with the toothpaste),
or a friend's death (That one, she didn't care
how sick she got, she always had her hair done),
his back pain, her arthritis, or the daughter
who won't diet (And she'd be such a beauty!);
after his joke about the nurse, and hers
about the bedpan, Listen, they each say,
Listen, what are ya gonna do?

                    'The Schmo,
he never should've married her, for Christ sake,
until he told her that he had a problem,
that was his first mistake, then he goes
throwing away his pills, because he's happy
he doesn't need them anymore, the schmo,
so of course what happens is she wakes up
and finds him weeping at the kitchen table,
just weeping, he doesn't know why, he won't eat,
won't get dressed, says he's quittin' his job,
you know, nuts, nuts, so naturally she leaves him,
the poor schmo, and he's such a good boy . . .'

90

All of the harm that's imperceptibly
but surely coming for them (the way the sun
burns brick by brick all morning toward the window
like a slow fuse) – all of the bad news now
is in the body only enough to hold
the middle sister's two hands open, shrug
her shoulders in a way they recognize
as hers, the way their mother did; as if
all trouble were, for now, no heavier
than the familiar voice repeating, Listen,
Listen it could be worse; So who's to say?;
What was, was; When your number's up – like old charms
woven around each story till they've made
what happens what was only meant to happen,
coherent with fate, fated as family.

After the funeral three months from now,
they'll have to listen to the older sister
tell them they had no business moving away
to Florida, and Irene sick as she was.
And selfish. She was selfish, that one. After
all those years of living with that bum,
her husband, may his cheap soul rest in peace,
didn't *she* deserve a little pleasure?
And anyway, what could be done for her?
Didn't the stroke just make it easier
for her to sit all day, and smoke, and not care
ashes were falling on the couch, the carpet;
her bathrobe filthy, filthy? Oh it was terrible –
and now they will hear the old unfairnesses,
old feuds and resentments come to her voice
like consolation, like a mother helping
her recite the story of that last bad day –
all that smoke, and running in with nothing
but the dishtowel to beat down the flames,
and Irene, just Irene, just sitting there,
the queen of Sheba – What difference did it make
since *she* was there, *she* was always there,
her big sister, to clean up the mess?

Only three months, and yet it could be years,
or decades, for the sun has only just now

91

caught in the window, and its bright plaque warms
the air so gradually that none of them
can know it's warming, or that soon someone,
distracted by a faint sheen prickling the skin,
will break the story, look up toward the window
and, startled by the full glare, check the time.
Right now, though, the future is a luxury
of instances in which the cigarette,
raised halfway to the lips, will go on rising.
Nothing bad, right now, can happen here
except as news, bad news the brother and sister
mull and rehearse, puzzle and fret until
it seems the very telling of it is
what keeps them safe. And safe, too, the oldest sister,
dreaming of all the perishables sealed,
wrapped up and hurried back into the fridge's
uncontaminated airlessness,
dreaming of how the soapsuds curdle and slide
over the dishes in a soothing fury,
not minding that it scalds her hands to hold
each plate and cup and bowl under the hot,
hard jet of water, if it gets them clean.

from

*Happy Hour*

(1987)

## Happy Hour

The gregarious dark is shifting
when she puts her second drink,
the free one, half on the coaster.
The tipped wine poised at the brim
is the beginning of the bad girl
she'll promise never to be again
tomorrow, who can taunt him now
to prove he doesn't love her
and never could: her hand slides
up his thigh until he tenses –
'My little prig, don't you want
to fuck me?' the bad girl
she couldn't be at home, his wife on ice.
All he can do is smile back
as though she's made a harmless
good-natured joke, and struggle
not to look around to see
who's heard, who's watching. He wants
to smash the wine glass in her face
so he can know for once
exactly what he's done wrong;
but he places it instead
back safely on the coaster
quickly before she sees.
Never cautious enough, he is prepared
even if she knocks it over
to go down on his hands and knees
and wipe it up, kind and forgiving.
In all ways careful to acquit himself
so that tomorrow when she says
she doesn't deserve him, he's too good,
he can believe her. Tomorrow
will be *his* happy hour. There won't be
anything she wouldn't do for him.

*Genie*


Though he would drink with her, he never drank as much
as fast, and often early on those evenings
she'd sense his stiff refusal as the gin fell.
Well, both had their parts, and needed them.
Honoring that need, she'd hurry along their words
from scene to scene, each more furious with meaning:
Neglected Wife and Disappointed Husband, the faithfully
directed tit-for-tats that always ended
with his back blurred in the glass as he'd dissolve to bed;
herself, at last, abandoned to her favorite role,
a genie in reverse; now she'd slip cleanly
into the snug hold of another bottle,
where she was rid of him, so she could grant him
what she knew must be his secret wish.

## Familiar Story

Tonight they need to be both host and stranger,
talking together all evening after dinner;
the candle wavering down till they are half
in darkness as they lead each other back
through their accumulated separated lore,
telling the stories they have told before
to other lovers, who are stories now.
They give no truth here, but the practised glow
of truthfulness: even as they confess
wholeheartedly to niggling attentiveness
disguised as love, to no or too much care,
affection parceled out till it's not there –
the more one tells, the more the other sees
just how appealing is this honesty,
how generous they are to those who hurt them.
They think this kind shrewd vision won't desert them.
And tonight, at least, it won't as they forget
what all their lore will lead them to expect
of one another, what they'll later owe
day after each slow day when all they know
is the familiar story they are living,
restless, and remote, and unforgiving.
It's then, when they don't feel it, they will need
the love bad days require and impede.
But not tonight, the candle going, gone,
their eyes shut briefly as the light goes on.
Tonight desire is generosity,
desire in each other's all they see,
and all else now is no more than the light
hurting their eyes, too sudden and too bright.

## The Riddle

Long ago, a little boy is winding up his soldier,
his concentration as deep as instinct as he turns
the brass key on the soldier's back easily at first,

then slowly, slower, twisting the key as far as it will go.
His mother at the stove in front of him is stirring
the huge pot steaming up into her face, and saying

over and over that he's a bad boy, a heart attack
he'll give her, is that what he wants? will that
make him happy? He is like the blue flames

under the pot, blue stars she makes appear
and disappear. He grips the key hard to keep himself
from going where her voice would send him,

his fingers reddening against it, beginning to tremble
as the coiled spring grows more eager, more insistent.
But he holds on, grips it harder; he's waiting

till he feels the poised soldier and his fingers merge
into a single yearning he can't hold back any longer,
till he needs to pull his hand away so badly

that it nearly feels like a bad thing to do.
The spring coils through him, knots and goes on knotting;
was it the blue flame he was reaching out to touch

that burned him then, or her hard hand slapping his?
The fire in her voice and on his hand all twisted now
as far as they will go, a riddle he can't solve

except to jerk his hand away as from another fire.
The key whirrs so furiously it disappears.
The soldier charges across the table toward his mother

and is just about to shoot her dead when he plunges
over the table's edge down to the floor
where the boy retrieves him, winds him up again,

grips him so his fingers burn, so the soldier can run
again like punishment against her, and again be punished
over and over for the bad thing he is about to do.

# A Christmas Story

*And the Lord said to Moses, 'When you go back to Egypt, see
that you do before Pharaoh all the miracles which I have put in
your power: but I will harden his heart, so that he will not let
the people go.'*
                              Exodus 4:21

It wasn't only envy but also a vague desire
to make amends, to glorify the baby Jesus
with my friend Charlie (who said the Jews had killed him)

that made me sneak into my parents' bedroom
Christmas morning before anyone was awake
to phone Charlie about all the presents

I hadn't received, the tree we didn't have.
Quietly as Santa (whom we must have also killed)
I took the phone down from my father's bedside table

and slipped under the bed into the cramped dark
of springs all intricately crossed and swollen
against me where my father slept. A long time

I lay there cradling the phone: I dialed
when either parent shifted or snored, afraid
that they somehow would answer at the other end:

or hear Charlie's father yelling 'Charlie make it quick'
and the forbidden prayer I whispered to him then
of every toy I had ever owned, or seen,

imagining that he imagined all of them right here
under a tree like his, and not the stark menorah,
our stunted version, with its nine thin candles

solemn as school, or the inkstand and underwear –
more chores than gifts – which I received for Chanukah.
No, it was Christmas here under my parent's bed,

100

it was His manger, and His death was as far from me
as I was from my own house carolling a holy
inventory to my friend. Then he was gone.

The springs became cold law against me as I was hauled
out clinging to the receiver like a hooked fish
to where my father waited, stern as the candles,

fisher of Jews; you want to be a goy, he said,
be a goy, and sent me to my room for the whole day
where it was Chanukah. And I was more a Jew

the more I pictured to myself all of the presents
I had seen at Charlie's house the day before,
a king's treasure, from which the tree ascended

in a pyramid of flames and glittering angels.
On my bare walls, all day, I had to build it
higher and brighter, as though it were a burden

I could not put down, could never escape –
driven to build it all day by a heart
the God of my father, the Lord our God, kept hardening.

## Rickshaw

Outside on the warped card tables all of her old things
seem hardly hers. They're almost new again out here
in this odd light, what she had grown so used to

and stopped seeing, or tired of seeing day after day on
the mantelpiece, coffee table, sill or shelf, and boxed and stacked
down in the basement far back in the dark corners, forgotten,

until today. Today they're all glittering with shadows
when the leaves stir. Today she should be happy.
Already she's made fifty, sixty dollars, maybe more,

the loose change in the pocket of her housedress now
so thick it no longer jingles when she moves, heavy
with the promise of what she'll buy. Why does it bother her

to see her neighbors gathered around the tables, chatting
softly as they pick up this electric knife, that necklace,
holding them out to her and asking, Will you take a dollar? . . .

Where in the world did you get this? someone asks,
pointing to an empty rickshaw planter which a little
chinaman is pulling – naked to the waist, and shoeless,

leaning forward with one leg slightly raised, his head bowed
and the wide-brimmed hat pulled down over his face so far
that only the blank line of his mouth is visible.

Where in the world? And suddenly she discovers how little
she can recollect of all the bright occasions – holidays,
or were they shopping sprees? – that carried so many things

year after year into her hands. Now in her neighbors' hands
they remind her of how she wanted them, how they were new
once, so free of her they let her go on wanting

even when they were hers; more promises than things,
glittering totems of their own arrival, they made all life
a present she forever opened until each became,

sooner or later, merely what all life was, a veteran novelty,
the trace of wishes that were vagrant as light,
tireless as the chinaman she takes another dollar for.

She puts her hand into the cool heavy change for reassurance –
her shoulders aching with what she's made – and sees a neighbor
leave with the rickshaw which the chinaman keeps pulling

out of the yard, across the street, drawing her home
to the mantelpiece, coffee table, sill or shelf where
he can keep on pulling the new plant she will surely buy.

*Extra*

The heart disease was worth it,
like a gorgeous blouse, expensive
but his favorite color,
like the last word on the subject
they've been arguing for twenty years.
Her friends had told her how
all week he was inconsolable,
how he wasn't sleeping and would cry
the two of them had wasted
all that time not speaking. He swore,
they told her in the private room
he insisted she should have
(though the insurance wouldn't cover it),
somehow he'd make it up to her.
And she answered, good, good.
From now on life would be his
making up to her, wooing her
the way he wooed her all week long,
visiting before work, after work,
each time with flowers, and the nurses
winking, whispering behind his back,
my, my, you have him trained.
For the first time since they moved out here
to start life over, she could think
happily about their new apartment;
the floor to ceiling chinese
lanterns casting an exotic twilight
through the living room, as though
the room were suddenly another
country she was touring through;
and the large white couches and white walls
streaked with a showering fireworks
of thousands of blue and yellow shapes
no two alike, all shimmering
in the glass coffee table
she almost didn't like to use

so it would seem new always,
something no one had ever touched –
it was a Jerusalem of tastefulness,
making their old life back east
a shabby makeshift exile.
But he worried everything, he nagged
dogged as a bill collector;
she was spending too much, why
an apartment with a pool? His whole life
working himself sick so that he'd have
a little extra for a sick day.


Today, though, as she waited for him
to take her home, she remembered
that the detective show on TV
which shot a scene by their pool
would be on tonight, and they would
watch together. She was an extra.
At the far end of the pool in a lounge chair
she had followed their directions, telling
all about her latest trip
to Acapulco as she murmured
rutabagas, rutabagas, rutabagas
to the woman next to her, who said back
peas and carrots, both of them
almost gawking as the star,
an undercover cop, strolled past them
to the beautiful bikinied girlfriend
of the mob boss he was after.
A woman from his past, she breathes
after the long heartbreaking
look of recognition, 'It's
been a long time since El
Paso,' and the scene was over.


Back up in the apartment, life
was no longer something that
happened somewhere else, to others.
She was near its rich
stunning heart, she was someone
who belonged, the kind of person

the apartment promised she could be.
But then when he came home and
sat down on his side of the bed,
his back to her, and started
to polish his golf shoes
because, he said, he had an early date
tomorrow on his day off,
and he was beat, and didn't want dinner –
when she stood there, hearing
the lavish wingbeat of the cloth
against the one shoe in his lap,
and staring at the other on the bed
beside him, facing the little
mud streaked spikes, the large
dumb back that never turned,
not even when she walked out,
she realized, she thought for good,
that to tell him anything, anything
at all that had to do with her,
would be to tell him rutabagas,
peas and carrots . . .
                              Yet here he was now
carrying her bags down to the car,
opening the door for her, and asking
almost shyly, like a newlywed,
if she were comfortable, could he do
anything, just name it honey.

Later that day, since he was snoring,
she got up for a cup of coffee.
She was thinking, though the doctors
warned her not to do too much,
that maybe she'd fix him a little
something, when she found a slum
of dishes in the sink, the refrigerator
empty, no coffee, no milk – in the dull
refrigerator glare nothing
had ever seemed so desolate, and yet
fulfilling in a way as she rushed back
breathless, yelling why the hell
hadn't he shopped, or cleaned up?
What was he doing all week?

106

And he bit back, making a goddamned living.
It was fulfillment of a kind,
the closest she could ever really
get to pleasure, as she got dressed
saying nothing while he stood there,
saying nothing though he followed her
out to the car and pleaded, honey,
make a list and I'll go shopping,
please, honey, let me go . . .

She could still hear him as she drove off.
In the rearview mirror he grew
smaller and smaller, as though seen
through the wrong end of a telescope,
through the sharpening lens of spite
that made him smaller, the clearer he became.
And she was almost sorry, sorry for them both
because she knew she would never again
give up this clarity. It was easier,
she knew now, to forget his brief
vagrant lapses into care
than to resist ever again the hard
current of their long past
which carried her now up and down
the aisles of the supermarket,
remembering all of the old complaints,
how if it shines, she'd buy it,
how she's never learned to live
within their means – she remembered
all of it and pulled down only
the dullest cheapest canned goods;
generic coffee, oily tuna, all
the frozen dinners she could find
until the cart was heavy
with everything he ever wanted.
And as she pushed it, her dress damp
and cold against her, she could feel
the blood ram through the clogged arteries
and the yellow bruise on her hip
from the angiogram begin to ache
so much that she imagined it was
flashing to the check out girl and

to the boy who lugged her eight bags
to the car that she was old and sick.

Her whole life seemed like one rehearsal
for this long drive home with groceries,
clenching the wheel to keep from fainting,
past none of the famous houses to
her own place, where he was waiting.
What do you want from me, he said,
what? what do you want?
But she wasn't done with him, not yet.
She dragged bag after bag up the stairs
through the living room aswim
in a crazy dream of colors
which only tired her now.
And she was still not done, not even
after she put everything away,
washed every dish, and was so weak
she had to let him help her back to bed.
For later he would wake her saying, honey,
don't you want to watch your show,
your show is on, honey, and she would
roll over, tell him she was
too beat, yes, she would make sure
that this last disappointment
and the regret she gives back in return
will be a final understanding
it has taken them their whole lives
to perfect, a sterling intimacy
that she will never, ever let him tarnish.

## Astronomy Lesson

The two boys lean out on the railing
of the front porch, looking up.
Behind them they can hear their mother
in one room watching 'Name That Tune',
their father in another watching
a Walter Cronkite Special, the TVs
turned up high and higher till they
each can't hear the other's show.
The older boy is saying that no matter
how many stars you counted there were
always more stars beyond them
and beyond the stars black space
going on forever in all directions,
so that even if you flew up
millions and millions of years
you'd be no closer to the end
of it than they were now
here on the porch on Tuesday night
in the middle of summer.
The younger boy can think somehow
only of his mother's closet,
how he likes to crawl in back
behind the heavy drapery
of shirts, nightgowns and dresses,
into the sheer black where
no matter how close he holds
his hand up to his face
there's no hand ever, no
face to hold it to.

A woman from another street
is calling to her stray cat or dog,
clapping and whistling it in,
and farther away deep in the city
sirens now and again
veer in and out of hearing.

The boys edge closer, shoulder
to shoulder now, sad Ptolemies,

the older looking up, the younger
as he thinks back straight ahead
into the black leaves of the maple
where the street lights flicker
like another watery skein of stars.
'Name That Tune' and Walter Cronkite
struggle like rough water
to rise above each other.
And the woman now comes walking
in a nightgown down the middle
of the street, clapping and
whistling, while the older boy
goes on about what light years
are, and solar winds, black holes,
and how the sun is cooling
and what will happen to
them all when it is cold.

from

*The Courtesy*

(1983)

# On the Eve of the Warsaw Uprising

*At the end of the Passover service, a cup of wine is set*
*aside for the prophet Elijah. The messenger of God, he is*
*appointed to herald the era of the messiah.*

*Elijah come in glorious state*
*For thy glad tidings long we wait.*
*Ah me, ah me, when cometh he?*
*Hush! In good time cometh he.*


My uncle said, 'This is Elijah's wine.'
Till then I mimicked listening, wide-eyed
with piety, while underneath the table
I kicked my brother back for kicking me.
The bitter herbs and the unleavened bread
that my uncle said were meant to make me feel
the brick and mortar, and the hurrying
between the walls of water that wind held back –
to me meant only an eternity
of waiting while he prayed, before a meal.

But when that wine was poured, the door left open,
waiting seemed almost holy: a worshipper,
the candle flame bowed in the sudden draft.
And for a moment I thought I'd behold
Elijah's glad lips bend out of the dark
to brighten and drink up into His Light
the Red Sea in the glass
                                          that never parted.
For soon my uncle closed the door when we
grew cold, and the flame straightened. 'Where was Elijah?'
Nobody in the room had ever asked.

And now I think, knowing what I know,
if anyone had ever come to us,
he could have come only to keep watch
and not to drink; to look upon the glass,
seeing within the wine, as from across
the whole of night, the small flame still as God;
someone who would have known the numberless
doors that have been opened, to be closed;
the numberless who watched till they became
the shimmer in the wine he looked upon.

## The Courtesy

*(for Saul Chessler, 1953-1974)*


I walked from my house down Coolidge Street last night
And air, beginning movement in the trees,
Shook down a hushing from the branches.
On either side of me the houses
Like solid shadow, blocks of silence
In the violet light, so dim without dimming.
And I saw you, Saul, my old friend, waiting
For me at the corner where our two streets met.


I wanted to ask you what it was like to die
But you said first, as if you didn't want to tell me,
'The doctors made me better. We can run again.'
You ran behind me (the way you always did),
Your slow strides lunging; though they never could keep up
This time they stayed right there at my heels.
Turning, I saw one pocket inside out
Clapping on your coat front like a white hand.
Your breath quickened, scrawled in the chilling air
Like mine, and vanishing. We ran on a field of snow.
Our footsteps pattered the smooth crust,
Each one feeling like it might break through.
Around us the pure white kindled under violet.


And we returned by train. Sitting next to you,
Staring through the window, I saw your body
Lying like a dark slash in the snow,
Your arms flung up, your legs crossed,
Even as I heard you next to me
Still struggling to catch your breath. You were just
Pretending to be alive – remembering to breathe.
Lumbering under living weight, saying you were cured,
Your flushed cheeks – all just to put me at my ease,
Afraid that your death might embarrass me, even then
Saul, you were more a friend to me than you were dead.
But in my mind the question was still circling:
What is it like to die? But how could I catch you

In a lie which you intended as a kindness?
Beside you on the train, hurtling back
Into the strange familiarity of Coolidge Street,
Remaining silent, I returned the courtesy.

## Yahrzeit

Each year my father has another soul
to pray for, another anniversary
of another's death, someone else to love
belatedly. Today it's his brother,
Amos, who died hating him and being hated.
Still my father stands here
bent over the little candle flame, swaying.
He can feel the old estrangements, the golden calf
of grievances their anger forged and worshipped
softening in these words, melting at last
to this barely articulated rise and fall,
more moan than prayer. It's as though his own loss,
his real brother, had become the wick
of this anonymous, inextinguishable sorrowing
whose pure heat, burning what he knows,
gives back to him unhindered love, another
family, a brother who can hear him now
and would have prayed for him, and loved him
as he never did, as his brother's brother
here in these syllables, if no where else.

## What Makes You Think It's Fear

Each morning from the house he sees the cat
who won't come near him, entering the garden.
It moves along the fencetop, through the ivy,
making the sounds of someone keeping quiet,
making him listen.
                        He wonders what it fears:
what makes it leap away when he goes out –
to perch on the far corner of the fence,
its paws drawn under it, the tail pulled round
like a moat?
                        In time the cat will stay, he thinks,
in time learn how mistaken its fears are.
He brings an offering to prove he's kind,
holding out to it a bowl of food,
shaking the bowl to prove that it is full
and not a trap,
                        calling out sweet names.
But far into the leaves the cat retreats
before it disappears; its green eyes glaring
and yet with no alarm, as he approaches,
holding the bowl and, almost fearful,
                                        calling,
calling out as if he asks for alms.

## First Night

If not relaxed that night,
we were, at least, not quite
that nervous; awkward, yes,
yet our uneasiness
became a kind of ease;
the way rain in the trees,
after a rain, is kept
by each impediment
from falling, as it falls.
So we'd advance, and stall,
fearing to show off, or
wishing we'd offered more –
until each courtesy
of pleasure let us see
how easy it is to praise
touching in all our ways;
with great or no aplomb,
with old hands, or all thumbs.

## Love Letter

Today, a soft rain
brings all outside near:
clear globes blur the trees
to a green atmosphere.

Evening lasts all day.
And through the house some
power comes, aimless,
calm, and you become

altered, a woman
I no longer know,
whom I may guess at,
whose attractions grow

as you grow more vague.
In this weather there's
something I should fear,
but can't; this rain stirs,

bringing its dark haze
down through trees; through me
darkening into
safe obscurity,

till even thoughts of you,
your hands' kind gestures,
seem like commands, your
softest touch, pressure

I can't bear. Feeling
just self-regard, and,
unafraid, I'm scared:
Dear, when will this end?

this rain chilling me?
Bring love's hard light home –
come back to where I,
knowing you, am known.

## Moving Day

Moving the furniture –
last relics of what they
together had arranged –
outside, out of the way,
he finds, because familiar,
the house becoming strange.

He rubs from bare white walls
the fog of webs, the scuff
of insects that he killed
and left, that added up
as if a kind of scrawl
whose meaning he now stills.

So cleaning house becomes
forgetting, as he cleans;
a covering of tracks
in an otherworldly gleam,
where no one's ever come,
where nothing stains, or cracks;

where perfect, for a time,
each sound inhabits quiet –
the dust is light that rains,
and hangers from the closet
chime from across a distance
no house could contain.

## Harvesting

We watched the lemons through the spring and summer,
small planets turning out of their green night
so slowly that we knew it would be winter
before we'd gather in that yellow light.

And, unaware, we shared as slow a ripening.
As quietly as lemons turning color,
our sweet days turned into remembering,
too swift a fragrance at the edge of anger.

And though it's winter and in the garden now
the lemons hang like worlds, forever day
for someone else, what weighed on other boughs
we harvest separately, and take away.

from

*After The Digging*

(1981)

## Randolf Routh to Charles Trevelyan

*– September 6, 1846*

Dear Sir, the harvest, such as it will be,
will be here soon. Yet we know it is Summer
only by the calendar. The rain
falls in unebbing tides, making each day
a darkness that the light illuminates.
Sir, the reports which come in every day
are not, as you suggest, exaggerations:
from Giant's Causeway to Cape Clear, from Dublin
to Galway Bay, the cold fires of disaster
burn through the green fields and each black plant blooms
luxuriant as an abundant harvest.

The people do starve
                              peaceably, as yet.
But how much longer, how much longer?
                                                        Armed
with spades, a horde of paupers entered Cork –
'So thin,' the officer in charge has written,
'I could not tell which ones were men, and which
were spades, except the spades looked sturdier.'
They demanded food, and work. And when dispersed,
'Would that the government would send us food
instead of troops,' one of them muttered, while
the rest like phantoms in an eerie silence
went off.
                Last week, outside of Erris where
the poor like crows swarm, combing the black fields,
living on nettles, weeds, and cabbage leaves,
women and children plundered a meal cart,
fifteen of them tearing at the sacks;
enlivened rags, numb to the drivers' whips,
too weak to drag the sacks off, or to scream,
they hobbled away, clutching to themselves
only small handfuls of the precious stuff.

Please do not think me impudent. Like you
I feel no great affection for the Irish.
But it is not enough that 'we should tell them

125

they suffer from the providence of God';
or that 'in terms of economic law
it's beneficial that the price of grain
should rise in proportion to the drop in wage'.
We can no longer answer cries of want
with quoting economics, or with prayer.
Ireland is not, and never can be, Whitehall.
And while they starve, no Englishman is safe.

Sir, you have said yourself, 'The evil here
with which we must contend is not the famine,
but their turbulent and selfish character,'
which I half think Nature herself condemns:
today, as if from the Old Testament –
with thunder beating on the iron clouds
which do not bend – the electricity
strikes with the bright and jagged edge of judgment,
while over each blighted field a dense fog falls
cold and damp and close, without any wind.

## The Dublin Evening Mail

*– December 6, 1846*

*CLARE*
This afternoon a gruesome incident,
not unfamiliar in these parts, occurred:
Captain Wynne's Inspector of the Works,
a Mr Pearson Hennessey, incurred
near fatal wounds as he approached Clare Abbey.
He was accompanied by his chief clerk
and five foot soldiers – three in front of him
and two behind – when a man dressed in a skirt,
with blackened face, walked slowly from a ditch
and fired his blunderbuss at Hennessey,
who fell back in great torture.
                                         The man bowed,
or rather as the clerk reports, curtsied
telling the others, 'I mean *ye* no harm.'

Shocked by his monstrous crime, and almost gay,
disarmingly good manners, no one tried
to apprehend him as he walked away.
Yet, fearing to be shot themselves, they ran
while Mr Hennessey, without assistance,
with eighty shots lodged in his body, crawled
into the village.
                        And the peasants danced
as if it were a circus that approached,
aplauding the poor man like fiends in hell,
and, when he pleaded for a doctor, joked
'Sure, now ye are a beggar like ourselves.'

## Captain Wynne to Randolf Routh

*– December 24, 1846*

Dear Randolf, since the shooting incident
my staff is greatly agitated, and
I fear won't hold together for much longer.
They all seem waiting for the right excuse
to go – Tom Webb has gone and his successor,
Mr MacBride (whom those who still can curse
call Mr Hennessey), has left already.
Mr Pratt's resigned, and Mr Gamble
(the engineer in charge) thinks Millet's life
is threatened, and is going to remove him.

We must resume the works. Though this suspension
be the only armor we possess
against the bullets of assassins, still
something must be done. I have myself
inspected the small hamlets in the parish
and would describe to you what I have witnessed,
but anything you picture to yourself
which still enables you to kiss your wife,
embrace your son, and sleep until you wake,
is not what I have seen, nor what I felt.
But I must tell you something nonetheless.

Since even nettles now have all been eaten,
or buried in the snow – the snow which now
alone must feed the peasants, and keep them warm –
each hamlet is entirely deserted.
I counted fifteen corpses on the road,
like crops the living were too weak to plant:
the only earth upon them was the snow,
a few sticks, and small stones.

                              And no sounds came
from any of the hovels that I passed.
And it occurs to me, in retrospect,
that those poor wretches must have heard me coming
and knowing that (as I must now confess)
I looked upon starvation as disease,

128

kept quiet as a trap to draw me in,
hoping to sicken me. And I was sickened:

In one small hut I saw six human beings
crouched in a corner in some filthy straw:
four had once been children, but now wore
the anxious look of premature old age;
the other two, their parents I presume,
for though as thin as children, they were taller.
As I approached I realized the father
was the only one alive, for he was moaning
low and demonically, and his legs twitched –
though not enough to move, or move the others
who leant upon him still as if in death
they still cried for the help he could not give.

I hurried off, and faces stared at me
from every window that I passed, faces
whose eyes hunger had magnified, whose lips –
the last soft flesh upon them – were as blue
as the new snow and were speaking God knows what,
soundless as in a dream . . . what were they speaking?
Tell me, Randolf, what words they uttered, words
which every night are riddling my dreams,
which I wake up to; tell me what they mean.

And tell me when the works will be resumed.
Consider, Randolf, what I have recited:
I am a match for almost anything
I meet with here, but this I cannot stand.
Consider it, for something must be done.
And trust I speak sincerely when I say
I hope the winter finds you well, and please
pass on warmest regards to Randolf Junior,
and kiss your dear wife once for me.

                                    Yours, Wynne.

## Passage Out

*(The log of Thomas Preston, captain of the brig* Temperance
*carrying Irish emigrants to Canada in the year of 1847)*

### JUNE 1

This good wind which has not let up
makes reaching Canada in six
or seven weeks conceivable.
And for our tattered Irish cargo
I pray we do. Our food will not
last any longer. As it is,
each person gets but seven pounds
of meal a week, which I have had
to ration daily. For I fear
these passengers, already being
in such a wretched state, would surely
consume at once all their provisions.

Almost none of them seem fit
for any travel. Most were sick
when we embarked, and some were starving.
Yet all were medically examined,
if one can call it that. They filed
one by one in quick succession
before a window, from which a doctor
glanced at their tongues, and took their money.
So frightened were they, filing past
with their tongues out and eyes shut tight,
it almost seemed they were receiving
communion and not passage out.
And yet so destitute perhaps
the only grace they now expect
is passage out.
    The brig itself
seemed like the new world they were seeking
as they climbed slowly up the planks,
up to the deck and, from the railing,
waved triumphant to their loved ones
whose cries rose up as much from fear
as grief, because they stayed behind
to turn back, exiled, to their homes.

## JUNE 7

Every day, from four to seven,
they come out of the hold and bicker,
crowding around the wooden stove
like gulls around a midden heap.
The ones with salted meat or herring,
the wealthy ones, keep frantic guard,
scalding their hands on the bright coals,
pushing the other hands away;
while the weak ones curse them to the grave
and shove till they are beaten back,
till they can grab their own turn, and
push back those weaker than themselves.
The young, the old, the most infirm,
mere rivals for each other's food:
even a pregnant woman – cursed
for the space her belly occupied –
was struck so hard that my first mate,
he had to bring her to my wife
who tends her now, free of her kin.
For there's no kin from four to seven,
no 'Irish' fighting at the stove –
just creatures who are suffering.
And then at seven from the shrouds
Jack pours some water on the fire,
and from the steam's hot surf they take
their half-cooked food down to the hold.


## JUNE 12

Kittens. Today I think of kittens,
my cousin Dorothy's when she
was but a child. Her cat had littered
four kittens among which there was one
identical to all the rest
except the grain across its tongue
turned out, not in. So everything
it tried to eat with all its might
sucking at its mother's teat,
sucking for its life,
                    that grain forbid.

131

And for the two days till it died
the sweet milk stained its muzzle white.
Dorothy asked, 'How could God do
such things?' And I cannot recall
how I replied. But I can guess,
today, what I would say to her.

Our water's running low: two casks
have started leaking and a third
which (now we know) held wine has turned
the water into vinegar.
Thus, I've had to reduce our rations.
And those with salted food – their last
remaining wealth – though they must starve,
have had to throw it overboard
for eating it brings on a thirst
their water cannot satisfy.

In the distant sky, all afternoon
we saw great combs of rain appear
and vanish, and appear, too far
for hope, yet too close not to see.
Then later the wind stopped.

                        And now
the ocean stiller than a pond,
marooned, I hear her ask that question
and I know what I would say to her.


*JUNE 20*

Ship fever, faster than a fire,
has broken out. And over fifty
of the hundred shut up in the dark,
unventilated hold are dying.
The 'Mistress', as my wife is called,
tends whom she can but can do little.
More than to ease their agony,
she quiets it, with laudanum.
Still. 'Mistress, please, for God's sake, water'
rises with the effluvium,
the shroud of stench that can be seen,
but not breathed, covering the deck.

## JUNE 23

A deputation came on deck,
fifteen or more, demanding water
for their sick ones below. Said they
would rush the store and help themselves;
'Are we to drink the diarrhoea?'
As helpless as they were enraged,
most could not even make a fist
or raise their arms.
                              One cruel mate seeing
but a relief from tedium
laughed at their threats and, for form's sake,
fired his gun into the air.
And the great bang hit them like a shot.
Some fell down to their knees, and begged;
the rest turned, climbing through the hatch
meekly, to face their families.


## JUNE 27

The dead are going overboard
without prayer, and with little sorrow
(for few have life enough for grief).
Like spoiled meat, husbands, wives, and children
thrown overboard into the deep –
as if this were their last kind act
that now they can relieve their kin
who have at last when they lie down
some room to change position in.


## JULY 9

At noon a brig about two miles
off starboard bow came into view.
And I am sure we looked to them
as they to us: serene against
the glister of the soft, green waves,
sunlight glinting off the bow,
the sails like blossoms on the wind
full as the white clouds, and as new.

## JULY 30
### Gross Isle, Canada

The foul mattresses, huge barrels
of vilest matter, the rags and clothes
dumped from the ships that came before us,
dumped in this river that is now
undrinkable, this water we
for weeks have dreamed of.
                              When we anchored
the doctor came on board and said,
'Ha, there is fever here,' and left.
And since then, now almost a week,
only the dead are brought to shore.
The rest must wait till there is room
for quarantine.
                              So from the brig
we watch while large and graceful ships
from Germany glide past with ease
bearing the robust passengers
on to their precious days. Cruel
the way they sing, the girls who laugh –
their blond hair shining in the sun –
laughing as they blow kisses to
those blighted shades who stagger out
of the dark hold, pained by the light.


## AUGUST 10

After the digging, Sean McGuire,
his skin too papery to sweat,
drove two shovels into the ground
making a cross, and said, 'By this,
Mary, I swear I will go back
as soon as I earn passage home
and murder him that murdered you,
our landlord, Palmerston.'
                              And went,
like all the rest, like living refuse
half naked, maimed to Montreal,
to Boston, to New York; the seeds
of typhus already blossoming.

And blossoming those other seeds
as virulent as a disease,
that grief which suffering can't feel,
that will return as surely as
the seasons when the flesh returns.
Who have endured must now endure
a healing no less unbearable,
must be consoled by hate's cold feel
fixing all their memories
into a purpose stronger than life,
immutable as loss.
                 They go,
and may God go with them who bring
into the new world nothing else
but epitaphs for legacies.

## Hands of Compassionate Women:
## Lam. 4, 10

Good friends and neighbors, I have come to tell you
(for I can see this now, now that I see)
that my intolerable twilight's over,
dissolved just as the Lord intended always.
Though palsied with the love I bore my child,
its small elusive good, I somehow felt
hope rising like the erratic exaltation
of larks in that vast pause before a storm.
But now all hope is stiller than a flame
no breathing frets. And I am almost calm
and, in a way, upright.
                              Oh how I hoped
then as I watched my child thrive day by day,
her flesh soft as a light upon her bones,
the warm light of the Lord. And so at first
I, loving her, praised Him. I prayed that since
she was so godly, surely I was God's,
surely He made my love His dwelling place.
And then the thought, as quiet as the quick
stealth of a thief, took shape in me, that He
could not love Jesus more than I loved her.
Then all my praising stopped.
                                          My child sickened,
faded with judgment, grew well like a sign,
shifted from His dark Word to His light
and back again. I drew back from her cries
as from a devils' chorus, hymning of sins
so deep they never could be named, or known.
I prayed myself to sleep each night and dreamt
another child, peevish because neglected,
tugged at my sleeve until I noticed him

136

who when I turned to notice turned away.
Throughout that awful twilight my little babe
was but the scripture of God's mood toward me,
the righteous reflex of a righteous love –
was hard and crooked where I was perverse,
shifting in and out of Hell, until today.
For I awoke, sensing a certain sweetness,
a kind of grace, and knew my trial was ending.

I have been cast out of God's furnace now,
as He once cast the child out of my loins,
much as I cast the child, my only hope,
my only child, this morning, into a well.
But I have come to tell you, you good people,
that when I heard her small weight hit, her one
brief cry, I felt – as you may never feel –
that what He hath intended hath been done,
and praised Him for the light He took away,
and praised Him because I knew, at last, that I
was damned, and that the dark was comforting.

## Night Seasons:
## The Captivity of Mary Rowlandson

*(Taken by the Wamponoags under King Philip in February, 1676,
and restored three months later.)*

> *I will make my arrows drunk with blood,*
> *and my sword shall devour the flesh –*
> *with the blood of the slain and the captives,*
> *from the long-haired heads of the enemy.*
> – Deuteronomy 32, 42

When Indians descended on your town,
emerging from the tree bark and the leaves
in a thick hail of bullets, hatchets, spears
glittering and swift, howling with awful joy –
it was the wilderness itself, ungodly,
sent of God, that came for you. It was
your Egypt, Goodwife Rowlandson, your time.
To His hard mercy God had called you out.
And seeing your house burn, children scattered, feeling
blood running down the daughter clinging to you,
you felt your faith turn at His call into
a hammer that could not let up, that worked
over and over at everything He sent you.
Nothing occurred that you did not deserve
or was not just: at even your poor babe's
'I shall die, I shall die' you struck and struck
till lying with her corpse all through that night,
not letting go until they stripped her, stiff
and blue, out of your arms, you thought how once
you could not bear the sight of death, and now
even its smell was sweet and savory.

You waited on the Lord by waiting on
your captors, sewing in exchange for food:
horse hoof or ear, a fawn so young its bones
were meat. In even the flintiest bread, in mould,
tree bark, or skunk you looked for God, to taste
His grace. And His Word, which you fed upon,
would bring in one hand, honey from the rock
of what you ate and leave you, in the other,
fed and unsatisfied, blood on your mouth.

Through the wild waters of the world, forsaken,
and gathered, and forsaken again, by Him
whose thoughts were not your thoughts, nor His ways yours,
you would forget inside the master's wigwam
and, dreaming upon the past, would suddenly
run out to your loved ones, the Christian world
in which you thought you had walked righteously,
finding only those devils, thick as trees,
yourself among them, searching for the sins
for which the Lord's Hand touched you, in His way.

He brought you home when you were ready. Then
and ever after, working in your thoughts
through each night season of the night, you felt
Him whose eye waketh ever, watching you.
You learned the vanity of things too well.
So with your family fast asleep about you
you must have thought of them, through your wild tears,
what careless thoughts their smallest dreams released;
heard each insect ticking in the wood
with much too dry a sound; and must have known
'afflicted' was the meaning of salvation,
knowing that you had been, and were, and would be
loved because chastened, scourged because received.

# SELECTED POEMS
## 1974-1996